T0316664

Cambridge Elements ≡

Elements in the Politics of Development
edited by
Melani Cammett
Harvard University
Ben Ross Schneider
Massachusetts Institute of Technology

 MIT CENTER FOR INTERNATIONAL STUDIES

PARTICIPATION IN SOCIAL POLICY

Public Health in Comparative Perspective

Tulia G. Falleti
University of Pennsylvania

Santiago L. Cunial
University of Pennsylvania

CAMBRIDGE
UNIVERSITY PRESS

CAMBRIDGE
UNIVERSITY PRESS

University Printing House, Cambridge CB2 8BS, United Kingdom

One Liberty Plaza, 20th Floor, New York, NY 10006, USA

477 Williamstown Road, Port Melbourne, VIC 3207, Australia

314–321, 3rd Floor, Plot 3, Splendor Forum, Jasola District Centre, New Delhi – 110025, India

79 Anson Road, #06–04/06, Singapore 079906

Cambridge University Press is part of the University of Cambridge.

It furthers the University's mission by disseminating knowledge in the pursuit of education, learning, and research at the highest international levels of excellence.

www.cambridge.org
Information on this title: www.cambridge.org/9781108468206
DOI: 10.1017/9781108622530

© Tulia G. Falleti and Santiago L. Cunial 2018

First published 2018

A catalogue record for this publication is available from the British Library.

ISBN 978-1-108-46820-6 Paperback
ISSN 2515-1584 (online)
ISSN 2515-1576 (print)

Participation in Social Policy

Public Health in Comparative Perspective

DOI: 10.1017/9781108622530
First published online: October 2018

Tulia G. Falleti
University of Pennsylvania

Santiago L. Cunial
University of Pennsylvania

Abstract: Health is a defining feature of life and its politics vital. Governments around the world and international organizations have promoted community participation in public health since the late 1970s. However, we lack comparative studies of these participatory institutions in public health. This Element proposes a conceptualization of *programmatic participation* and distinguishes between two types: one oriented toward *monitoring* and another oriented toward *policy making*. Falleti and Cunial review the origins of state-sanctioned institutions that mandate community participation in health in the two world regions with the most advanced social welfare systems: Western Europe and Latin America. This implies a comparative analysis of eleven health care systems. They argue that the origins of participatory institutions (whether rooted in administrative or political reform processes) help account for the resulting types of programmatic participation. They also delve deeper into the study of an experience of participation for policy making, and analyze two hundred local participatory projects in public health carried out in Argentina in the late 2000s. This allows them to focus attention on the characteristics of participants, the role of health care professionals, and the role of local politics in the execution of community projects. Falleti and Cunial conclude with their main findings and the contributions of their study to the literature on public health and participation.

Keywords: Participation, Public Health, Latin America, Western Europe, Health Council, Argentina, REMEDIAR, Proyectos Locales Participativos (PLP), Decentralization, Alma Ata

ISBNs: 9781108468206 (PB), 9781108622530(OC)
ISSNs: 2515-1584 (online), 2515-1576 (print)

Contents

The most important aspect of modern medicine is unquestionably that of Public Health, embracing as it does the four fundamental historical functions of the physician: to heal, to know, to predict, to organize. Félix Martí-Ibáñez, "Foreword," cited in Rosen (1957, 13–14)

Medicine is a social science ... Politics is nothing but medicine on a large scale. Rudolph Wirchow, cited in Rosen (1957, 13)

1 Introduction

Since the last quarter of the twentieth century and against the backdrop of democratization and market-oriented reforms, countries around the world have devolved fiscal resources, administrative responsibilities, and political authority to local governments (Grindle, 2000; Montero and Samuels, 2004; Willis et al., 1999). Even if the degree of power devolved to subnational authorities has varied widely across countries (Falleti, 2005, 2010a), subnational governments have acquired more political and policy salience. The sweeping wave of decentralization of governance resulted in the increasing importance of regional and local governments over the management, funding, and delivery of social services and local public goods. Throughout the world, local governments are not only responsible for water distribution, sewerage (where available), and garbage collection – the traditional responsibilities of local governments – but also for administering poverty alleviation and welfare programs, managing public primary education, and providing at least some primary health care services (Arretche, 1999; Souza, 2004; Weitz-Shapiro, 2008).

Decentralization has also facilitated civic participation at the local level (Goldfrank, 2007b). Around the world, local civic engagement has been advocated by both the political left and the political right, whether by design or by default (Baiocchi and Ganuza, 2017). By design, local, regional, and national governments (largely) on the left of the political spectrum have promoted participatory institutional innovations to increase citizen participation in public decision making and strengthen political incorporation (Goldfrank, 2011; Heller, 2001; Pogrebinschi and Samuels, 2014). By default, recurring financial and economic crises have turned local governments into the first trenches of heightened societal needs and demands (Wolford, 2010). After the adoption of neoliberal reforms, civic society participation to address problems with public goods management and social services provision has been functional to the withdrawal of the nation-state from many of its social welfare functions (Collier and Handlin, 2009; Ewig, 2010). Former Conservative British Prime Minister David Cameron dubbed this increased role of civil society in governance the "big society."[1] Interestingly, in the same way that decentralization reforms had been advocated by societal and political actors on both the left and the right of the political spectrum (the former pursuing democratization through political and fiscal decentralization, the latter seeking to shrink the state through administrative decentralization),[2] societal participation, too, has been advocated by social and political actors at opposite ends of the ideological spectrum in the pursuit of varying goals.

In political science, a growing literature exists on community participation, by which we mean the type of civic engagement activities that are outside what is generally understood as political participation, that is, voting, contacting a public official, contributing to a political campaign (Verba et al., 1995) and also outside what is conceptualized as social contestation (e.g., McAdam et al., 2001, Tarrow, 2008 [1998]). This type of civic participation is part of what scholars have alternatively called civic engagement (Putnam, 1993), social activism (Seligson and Booth, 1976, 97), volunteering (Schmitt, 2010, 1443), or programmatic associational participation (Dunning, 2009). Most of the recent literature on community participation, particularly as it pertains to the local level, has focused on the institution of participatory budgeting, an institutional innovation designed to include civil society in local investment decisions (Abers, 2000; Baiocchi et al., 2011; Goldfrank, 2007a; Sintomer et al., 2010; Souza, 2001; Tranjan, 2016; Wampler, 2007). Among international donors, community participation and monitoring have also been at the center of attention of researchers and program evaluators (Björkman and Svensson, 2009; Humphreys et al., 2012). Civic participation in educational councils (Altschuler and Corrales, 2012), security councils (Gonzalez, 2016), and water basin councils (Abers and Keck, 2013), among other local, regional, and national (Pogrebinschi and Samuels, 2014) participatory institutions has also been studied. Relatively less attention, however, has been paid to civic participation in public health, on which we will focus our empirical analysis.[3]

In fact, little attention has been paid to health politics within political science, despite the fact that health is a defining feature of life (Carpenter, 2012) and that minimal health conditions are necessary for human functioning

---

[1] On British Prime Minister David Cameron's project of "big society," see the series of articles featured in *The Economist*: "Big society: Radical ideas from a fusty old island," March 17, 2011; "What's wrong with David Cameron's 'Big Society,'" Feb. 10, 2011; "The Big Society. Platoons under siege," Feb. 10, 2011.

[2] For a conceptual and operational definition of decentralization that distinguishes among its administrative, fiscal, and political components, see Falleti (2010a, 33–39).

[3] The main exception is the case of Brazil, where an abundant literature exists on civic engagement in local health councils (see, among others, Avritzer, 2009; Cornwall, 2008; Labra, 2005). The field experiment by Björkman and Svensson (2009) also analyzes the effects of a community participation and monitoring intervention in health in rural Uganda.

in other realms such as citizenship, labor, education, consumption, reproduction, leisure, and spirituality (Sen, 1999). Moreover, civic participation in health systems is puzzling. Unlike the case of educational councils, for instance, where parents with children of school age interact with their children's schoolteachers and administrators on a regular (sometimes daily) basis, the average individual interacts far more sporadically with the health care system. Also, in many societies doctors have high social status prestige, knowledge, and power over quality-of-life decisions, even over life or death decisions, affecting their patients. Legitimated healers enjoy a particular legal authority and cultural power (Carpenter, 2012, 298) that intimidates a large portion of their patients, particularly those who are users of public health systems. Thus, on the account of both regularity of interaction and social hierarchy among doctors and patients, civic participation in health is unexpected or surprising, and its politics awaits further study.

In this Element, we comparatively study the origins and the initial legal regulation and implementation of participatory institutions in public health. The Element is organized in five sections. The next section advances our conceptualization of programmatic participation and our main argument: the origins of participatory institutions in health (i.e., whether they are born out of administrative or political reform processes) are strong predictors of the type of programmatic participation that results. In this section, we also engage with alternative arguments and describe our research design. The third section empirically applies our main argument, as it compares the institutional origins of participatory institutions in public health in eleven countries across Western Europe and Latin America. In the fourth section, we delve into an in-depth analysis of a participatory experience in Argentina, which allows us to tease out some of the characteristics of the process of institutional creation and evolution of programmatic participation in health. In the final section, we conclude by summarizing our main findings and the contributions of our study to the literature on public health and participation.

2 Programmatic Participation and Institutional Origins

Theoretically, we are interested in a specific type of civic participation: *programmatic participation*. To define programmatic participation, we draw from Booth and Seligson's definition of political participation as behavior oriented toward the distribution of public goods (Booth, 1979, 30–31; Booth and Seligson, 1978, 5–9) and from Davies and Falleti's definition of local programmatic participation as organized behavior that aims to influence the distribution or management of social services (Davies and Falleti, 2017, 1704). We define *programmatic participation* as "institutionally organized and state-sanctioned individual or collective behavior that influences or attempts to influence the management or distribution of public goods or social services," such as public budgets, schools, health clinics, or environmental protection. The fact that this participation (whether individual or collective) seeks to influence public goods or social services is central to our labeling it "programmatic." This is to say, this is not participation that seeks to gain individual access to services or goods, such as in the case of clientelistic exchanges where political support is provided to gain individual access to either public or quasi-market social services. Hence, it is worth reviewing the types of goods and services to which programmatic participation applies.

As defined by Olson (1968, 14), a *public good* is "any good whose consumption by any person in a group does not entail withholding of the good from others in that group." Or, as Cammett (2014, 268 n. 5) explains, "public goods are nonexcludable (i.e., those who have not paid for them can use them) and nonrivalrous (i.e., one users' consumption does not impede another's use of the good, at least not until consumption reaches a point of saturation)." Clean air, potable water, garbage collection and processing, road infrastructure, electricity infrastructure, telecommunication networks, public parks and recreation are all examples of public goods.

With regard to social services, as Cammett (2014, 12) explains:

> Welfare and social services encompass a wide array of policies designed to redistribute income and mitigate risk. These programs can operate through insurance schemes designed to cushion life-cycle and market-based vulnerabilities, such as ill health or unemployment, or through expenditures of basic services such as health care, schooling, or direct income assistance.

Unless there is perfect universal access to social services, they are excludable: they target certain sectors of the population under certain criteria, such as level of income, place of residence, citizenship status, employment status, and so on. Social services may also be rivalrous in that one person's or community's consumption of the good takes resources away from another person's or community's ability to enjoy it. Take, for instance, the decision over the construction of a local health clinic or the definition of its catchment: only those in the chosen community or catchment area will enjoy (whether de jure or de facto) the health services provided by that clinic. Finally, whereas either state or non-state actors can provide social services, for the purposes of this Element, we are primarily concerned with programmatic participation oriented toward social services provided by the state, and toward public health services in particular.[4]

---

[4] For excellent analyses of non-state provision of public services around the world, see Cammett and MacLean (2014).

Programmatic participation is voluntary behavior; but unlike broader definitions of civic engagement or volunteering, we are interested in programmatic participation that is *sanctioned, promoted, or at least institutionally recognized by the state, in any of its territorial levels (central, intermediate, or local).* In this volume, we focus our empirical analysis on programmatic participation that seeks to affect the design, management, and delivery of health care services in the public sector, particularly at the local level and in the context of health councils or committees that include civil society members. These health councils are examples of participatory institutions.

We follow the definition of *institution* proposed by Brinks, Levistky, and Murillo (2018, 7): "a set of formal rules structuring human behavior around a particular goal by (a) specifying actors' roles, (b) requiring, permitting, or prohibiting certain behaviors, and (c) defining the consequences of complying or not complying with the remaining rules." Participatory institutions, in turn, belong to what Graham Smith (2009, 1) has called *democratic innovations* – institutions "specifically designed to increase and deepen citizen participation in the political decision-making process." Or, as previously defined in collaborative research (Davies and Falleti, 2017; Falleti and Riofrancos, 2018), participatory institutions are formal, state-sanctioned institutions explicitly created to augment citizen involvement in decision making over public goods or social services. These institutions provide citizens with a normal politics means of interacting with the state and are potentially more substantive than sporadic electoral participation at the ballot box, while being less disruptive than social protest (Cameron et al., 2012; Fung and Wright, 2003). Examples of participatory institutions include, among others, participatory budgeting, water committees, local oversight committees, prior consultations, and health councils, on which we focus our analysis.

Building upon and combining insights from previous typologies of civic participation (in particular, Sáez González, 2013, 50; Anigstein, 2007), we distinguish between civil society's activities of consultation, planning, monitoring, and execution that can take place within participatory institutions in the public health sector.[5] *Consultation* refers to cases where the state disseminates

---

[5] Sáez González (2013, 50) distinguishes among advising, resolutive, and executive participation. Advising participation refers to those instances in which citizens can give their opinion on a specific issue (but this opinion is not binding for policy makers). Resolutive participation implies that citizens participate in the design of a public program and their opinions are binding. Finally, executive participation supposes taking part in the performance of an activity and/or in the provision of a service. Similarly, Anigstein (2007) proposes distinguishing among informative, advising, monitoring, and agenda-setting participation. Informative participation refers to those cases in which citizens are only informed about what the state is doing. Advising participation (as in the case of Sáez González's typology) entails those cases in which citizens can give their opinion on a specific issue. Monitoring participation is related to those cases in

information on a specific issue and/or invites the community to express an opinion on it. However, it is not mandatory for the state to implement the community's opinion. By *planning*, we refer to cases of community participation where the community's resulting decisions or outcomes of discussion or deliberation become a mandate for the state, which must translate those decisions into policies or practices. Planning activities often presuppose the act of prioritizing among possible outcomes or courses of state action in policy making. *Monitoring* is the third type of community participation and entails the community having the authority to evaluate the delivery of the public services or the execution of a certain policy. It is related to surveillance and accountability practices. In public social services, telephone lines or complaints books are sometimes designed to promote this type of participation (which can be exercised both individually and collectively). Finally, the fourth type of community participation, which we label *execution,* consists of community participation experiences in which citizens have the authority to execute or carry out a certain policy or program.

While exhaustive of the different functions that community participation may have vis-à-vis social policies and practices, these participation activities (consultation, planning, monitoring, and execution) are not exclusionary. In fact, as we show in the comparative empirical analysis in the next section, institutional designs for programmatic participation most often combine two or more of these functions. Consultation – as the act of the state providing information to civil society – is present in all institutional designs of participation in public health, but variation exists regarding the presence or absence of the other three types of activities.

We distinguish between two ideal types of programmatic participation. We label the first ideal type of participation *programmatic participation for monitoring*. In this type of participation, the main roles of civil society are to observe public officials and employees and to denounce them whenever they deviate from the prescribed or desired behavior. If authorities or employees at the local level, for instance, divert public money or resources, civil society is engaged through this type of participation to bring accusations to higher-level government officials. In this modality of participation, civil society is informed of projects, programs, and policies, but it does not provide feedback that is conducive to policy action. Participants receive and process information (consultation). They

---

which citizens evaluate and control public programs. Lastly, participation related to agenda setting refers to those instances in which citizens can put certain topics into the public agenda.

also monitor, becoming watchdogs or advocates and enforcers of accountability.[6]

The second ideal type is *programmatic participation for policy making*. This modality of participation entails collective or collaborative behavior, many times requiring face-to-face interactions and gatherings among participants. Participants collectively set communal priorities, plan social policies, or design programs (planning). All these activities presuppose the existence of at least a modicum level of deliberation and moderating mechanisms within participatory institutions. In this modality of participation, where civil society is highly engaged in policy making, civil society participants may consequently be invited or have the initiative to execute (at least in part) the designed policies and programs, often with the financial and technical backing of the state bureaucracy (execution).

These two ideal types of programmatic participation are directly related to what Carol Pateman (2012) identifies as the two modes in which democracies can engage the public in participatory innovations. According to Pateman,

> In a privatized social and political context in the twenty-first century, consumer-citizens need to be extra vigilant and to monitor providers; they require information, to be consulted, and occasionally to debate with their fellow consumer-citizens about the services they are offered. In contrast, the conception of citizenship embodied in participatory democratic theory is that citizens are not at all like consumers. Citizens have the right to public provision, the right to participate in decision-making about their collective life and to live within the authority structures that make such participation possible. (Pateman, 2012, 15)

As we survey the public health care systems around the world, and in particular in Latin America and Western Europe, that have instituted civic participation, our main contention is that *the type of programmatic participation observed in the health sectors' institutional innovations for civic participation* (whether those institutions are primarily oriented toward programmatic participation for monitoring or for policy making) *is the result of the administrative or political process behind their creation*. To put it succinctly, administrative reforms lead to participatory institutions for monitoring, while political reforms lead to participatory institutions for policy making.

By *political reform process*, we refer to the collection of political events taking place in the larger political system when the institutional innovations for participation in health are created. Political reform processes can entail events

---

[6] In fact, such accountability may be based in informal mechanisms and thus even operate in authoritarian regimes (Tsai, 2007).

as radical as those present in a social revolution (which as defined by Skocpol (1979) implies a complete transformation of the state and the economy) or those present in a political regime change (such as a transition from authoritarianism to democracy, or vice versa). Such changes can also entail more moderate events that are still significant from a public policy orientation perspective, such as a transformation in the balance of power among political parties and their social bases, which may imply a transition from governments based on right-leaning electoral bases and rightist policies to governments based on left-leaning electoral bases and policies (such as occurred during the period of the left turn in Latin America).

By *administrative reform process*, we refer to the collection of events that affect a particular policy sector (such as education, health, housing, pensions, etc.). Administrative reform processes are closely linked to ideas of *governance* reforms or transformations of the state's bureaucracy. This is to say, in the context of administrative reform processes, there are no radical changes in the state or the economy, in the type of political regime, or in the overall balance of power among political parties and societal actors.

We argue that where civic participation in public health is the result of administrative reforms of the health care system, institutions that promote programmatic participation for monitoring are most likely to be implemented. In cases where civic engagement in public health is the result of a broader political reform process that transcends the health sector (such as in the context of social revolutions, democratic transitions, or a "left turn" in politics), the resulting participatory institutions in health will promote programmatic participation for policy making.

These two types of programmatic participation are ideal types of different forms of civic engagement in public health. However, as we show in the next section, the institutions that promote civic engagement in public health operate in a continuum that goes from a minimum of only implementing consultation and monitoring activities (close to the ideal type of programmatic participation for monitoring), through an intermediate area in which planning is also included, to a maximum level of activities including consultation, monitoring, planning, and execution. This is to say, in practice, the participatory institutions that promote programmatic participation for policy making through the activities of planning and execution also include the less demanding (from a civil society's engagement point of view) activities of consultation and monitoring. It is also worth noting that our argument applies to the features of institutional design and its initial implementation through regulatory legislation. We do not attempt to account for institutional evolution through time, institutional strengthening, or institutional performance, which would require a different research design.

2.1 Alternative Explanations of Types of Participatory Institutions

Our comparative cross-national analysis of institutional designs for programmatic participation in public health systems (Section 3), as well our in-depth comparative analysis of local participatory projects in health carried out in Argentina during its left turn (Section 4) aim to dialogue and probe some of the political science and sociology explanations regarding two main questions: (1) What accounts for different types of participatory institutions? and (2) Who participates?

2.1.1 What Accounts for Different Types of Participatory Institutions?

The literature on participatory democracy has identified two causal pathways to the adoption of participatory institutions. First, participatory institutions may result from bottom-up mobilization and demands. In Porto Alegre, Brazil, for instance, participatory budgeting was initially a social movement proposal. It was adopted by the municipal government through a process of contentious interactions between neighborhood associations and the local administration as part of a broader set of institutional reforms centered on the democratization of the state, social justice, and economic redistribution (Baiocchi and Ganuza, 2015). Second, participatory institutions can be imposed from above, absent a demand from civil society, as was largely the case in Peru, Mexico, or in many instances of diffusion of participatory budgeting as "best practice." In these cases, studies have shown that participatory institutions do not fundamentally alter state-society relations and remain weakly institutionalized (see, among others, Hevia de la Jara and Isunza Vera, 2012, 80; McNulty, 2011; Zaremberg et al., 2017). Lindsay Mayka (2019) probes the question of institutional strength of participatory institutions more deeply: a participatory institution is strong when it has a proper and explicit institutional design, combined with high routinization and high infusion with value. For Mayka, sweeping sectoral reforms that change the status quo and thus allow for the formation of a broad reform coalition that in turn activates pro-participation policy entrepreneurs are the necessary conditions that combine to produce strong participatory institutions in health.

We believe similar causal dynamics apply to the type of programmatic participation taking place in the health sector. Our analysis of the secondary literature on participation in health reveals that when the social actors pushing for participation in health are closely linked to civil society (or have a history of working collaboratively, even if they are members of sectoral or bureaucratic elites), programmatic participation for policy making is more likely. Instead, when participatory institutions are imposed by administrative reforms and particularly by international donors, programmatic participation for monitoring is more likely. However, our argument does not perfectly map the idea of the reforms being implemented from above or below or with broad reform coalitions. It is important to emphasize that our dependent variable or outcome of interest is not institutional strength, but type of participatory institution. Thus, even if programmatic participation takes the form of participation for policy making, this does not necessarily imply institutional strengthening. The case of local participatory projects in health in Argentina, which were adopted extensively as an initiative from above, led by social scientists, doctors, and health practitioners with a progressive agenda and a history of participation with civil society, shows that they did not endure after political change. The program was institutionally weak, as it did not survive after its creators and first implementers left the national public administration. Yet, it was a case of programmatic participation for policy making.

The analysis of local participatory projects in health in Argentina (Section 4) also shows that, as in the case of other health reforms such as universalization of coverage, elites were instrumental. Similar to Harris's (2017, 4) findings regarding the processes of universalization of coverage in Brazil, South Africa, and Thailand, we also find that "'professional movements' of progressive doctors ... and other medical professionals with access to state resources" were key actors for the design and enactment of the participatory reforms. As Harris (2017, 4) writes, these are "elites from esteemed professions who, rationally speaking, aren't in need of health care or medicine themselves and who would otherwise seem to have little to gain from such policies," including participation. Their work with the poor, nonetheless, informed their advocacy for health reforms that would include community participation as a means to empower poor individuals, women in particular, and poor neighborhoods and communities. Similarly, Natasha Borges Sugiyama (2008) shows that Brazilian municipalities with authorities linked to a public health professionals association (*Centro Brasileiro de Estudos de Saúde*, CEBES) were more likely to adopt a primary care family health program (*Programa Saúde da Família*). And Mayka (2019) has also stressed the importance of pro-participation policy entrepreneurs to activate participatory institutional designs. Our empirical analysis is consistent with these findings.

However, two alternative explanations do not find support in our study. In her analysis of different participatory experiences around the world, Pateman (2012, 15) suggests that whereas engagement of participants as policy makers is present in the experiences of developing countries, engagement of participants as consumers is found in "rich" countries. Our analysis shows that engagement of citizens as consumers is also found in the developing world. While it is true that the three rich European countries of our sample (Italy, Portugal, and the Netherlands) instituted participation for monitoring, this is also the case in Colombia, a non-rich country. Thus, we believe there must be other causal dynamics that account for the type of programmatic participation promoted in public health that go beyond the geographic region or economic level of development of a country.

Second, it could be argued that our category of administrative reform process is in fact a proxy for neoliberal reforms, which would be the real cause behind programmatic participation for monitoring. While it is true that neoliberal ideas and policies oriented the reform agendas of all the countries that instituted programmatic participation for monitoring (Italy, Portugal, and Colombia in the 1990s, and the Netherlands in 2006), interestingly they also guided the sectoral reforms of Bolivia and Ecuador in 2002. Yet, both countries used those institutional frameworks (created in the neoliberal context) to promote programmatic participation for policy making in health once they were part of a broader political reform process, as shown in the next section.

2.1.2 Who Participates?

For a long time, the scholarly consensus in political science had been that citizens endowed with the highest levels of economic and social capital participate the most, whether in elections, in local institutions such as school boards, or even in community associations (Collier and Handlin, 2009; Putnam, 2000; Verba et al., 1995). In fact, in liberal democracies, one of the most systematic social science findings is that the participatory process exhibits a high-class bias that exacerbates socioeconomic inequalities (Verba et al., 1978; Verba et al., 1995, 186, 509–33).[7]

Such scholarly consensus started to develop more than fifty years ago, when as part of the behavioral turn in the social sciences, a prolific research agenda emerged on the individual predictors of political participation. Drawing from public opinion surveys, scholars focused attention mostly on developed societies, where individuals' attitudes and beliefs or their economic and social capital endowments were found to be largely accountable for their type and level of participation (Almond and Verba, 1963; Verba et al., 1995). Overall, individuals' income and education were powerful predictors of civic competence and participation (Almond, 1980, 23; Verba et al., 1995, 420).

---

[7] For an alternative account of participation in the United States, based on the concept of "issue publics," see Han (2009).

Meanwhile, the early research on political participation in nondemocratic or underdeveloped contexts yielded less uniform results (for a summary of these early research findings, see Booth, 1979, particularly pp. 32–45). As Davies and Falleti (2017, 1702) argue, these conflicting findings were largely the result of concept stretching: political participation was defined too broadly, encompassing electoral (voting, interaction with elected officials, and political party and campaign activity), community-oriented behavior (civic and social activism), as well as contentious (such as strikes, protests, riots, or land invasions) and noncontentious forms of participation (such as community improvement participation, organizational activism). Greater conceptual precision regarding political participation, operationalized as voter turnout, produced more conclusive results, whether the main focus had been on individual, institutional, or structural-level variables (Fornos et al., 2004; Pérez-Linán, 2001; Remmer, 2009). Studying local political participation in the rural villages of two Indian states, Krishna (2006) also finds that wealth does not matter for citizens' political participation. Thus, while the high-class bias explanation has been disputed in developing countries when applied to political participation and voter turnout, relatively little attention has been paid to the individual-level determinants of non-electoral and noncontentious modes of participation such as civic or community programmatic types of participation.

In the recent past, the eruption of participatory institutional innovations, particularly in Latin America, has allowed for a new wave of research on who participates. In one of the pioneering studies of participatory budgeting, Abers (2000) showed that those most in need were participating more in Porto Alegre, Brazil. Similarly, Davies and Falleti (2017) showed that in local community organizations such as neighborhood committees, school councils, and local economic associations, those with the lowest socioeconomic income and less education participated more in Bolivia, both before and after its left turn (which started in 2006). Do these findings extend to civic and community programmatic participation in health?

We address this question in our in-depth analysis of local participatory projects in public health in Argentina (Section 4). We find that participants are mostly poor. This is largely because the users of the public health system in Argentina, particularly in rural areas or in peripheral neighborhoods of cities, are largely from low socioeconomic status groups. Upper and middle classes in Argentina use private or social insurance health services and are rarely found among the patients of the primary public health clinics. In other words, the fact that this participatory program was embedded in the Argentine public health system meant that, by design, it targeted relatively poor communities and individuals. Moreover, our empirical analysis of local participatory projects in health in Argentina shows that women participate significantly more than men.

2.2 Civic Participation in Public Health

The 1960s saw the proliferation of community projects in health care (Sanabria Ramos, 2004). However, citizens' participation in health was not formally recognized as a right until 1978, when the World Health Organization (WHO) convened the International Conference on Primary Health Care, in Alma-Ata (USSR, now Kazakhstan). The Declaration of Alma-Ata established that participation was not only a right but also a duty to be exercised individually or collectively in the planning and implementation of health care. The Declaration also stated that health (which is defined as a state of complete physical, mental, and social well-being, and not merely the absence of disease or illness) is a fundamental human right and that the attainment of the highest possible level of health is a most important worldwide social goal whose realization requires the action of many other social and economic sectors in addition to the health sector (World Health Organization, 1978). During this conference, the WHO launched the goal "Health for all the people of the world in the year 2000" and defined the Primary Health Care as follows:

> Essential health care based on practical, scientifically sound, and socially acceptable methods and technology, made universally accessible to individuals and families in the community through their full participation and at a cost that the community and country can afford to maintain at every stage of their development in the spirit of self-reliance and self-determination. (World Health Organization, 1978, vi)

Community participation was one of the founding principles of Primary Health Care (Rifkin, 2009, 31–32). After the Declaration of Alma-Ata, community participation projects flourished, whether promoted by civil society or the state (Saez González, 2015), most likely in response to the conference's powerful advocacy for Primary Health Care (De Vos et al., 2009). By the mid-1980s, Susan Rifkin (1986) could already look back at 200 case studies of community participation since the start of that decade.

How should community participation in health systems be designed and implemented? As we show in the next section, state actions to either generate or respond to societal demands for greater participation have not been homogeneous. While some countries have promoted the involvement of citizens in the design and execution of public health policies (*programmatic participation for policy making*), other states have developed institutional frameworks oriented to listening to citizens' opinions and evaluations on public issues (*programmatic participation for monitoring*).

In what follows, we describe and compare programmatic participation in public health systems in the two regions of the world that have historically had the most advanced welfare states: Western Europe and Latin America.[8] Within each region, we analyze *all* the countries that have national- or regional-level legislation on civic participation in their public health care systems since the Declaration of Alma-Ata, and for which there is a sufficient body of literature that has analyzed them. In the case of Europe, these are Italy, the Netherlands, and Portugal. In the case of Latin America, the countries analyzed are Argentina, Bolivia, Brazil, Chile, Colombia, Cuba, Ecuador, and Venezuela.[9]

For the selection of cases, we searched all the secondary literature in the digital libraries JSTOR, Google Scholar, Scielo, PubMed, Taylor and Francis, SAGE, and Redalyc. In our searches, we looked for the terms "health participation," "participatory institutions," and "citizen participation" over a twenty-year period (1998–2018). We searched for articles published in English, Portuguese, and Spanish. Once these articles were collected, we focused our analysis on those country cases that presented participatory institutions sanctioned by the state (to conform with our conceptualizations of "participatory

---

[8] Since Alma-Ata, participation has also been promoted in other regions of the world, such as in Asia and Africa. In South Africa, for example, policy makers have sought to institutionalize community participation in Primary Health Care, recognizing participation as integral to realizing South Africa's constitutional commitment to the right to health. With evolving South African legislation supporting community involvement in the health system, early policy developments focused on Community Health Committees as the principal institutions of community participation (Meier et al., 2012). In Asia, most governments have promoted participation in program management (operational planning, monitoring of health delivery, managing of infrastructure, and user fees' collection), but not in design or policy formulation (Murthy and Klugman, 2004, 81). Exceptions to this trend, however, exist in some countries where community participation was sought in the design of the reforms or in setting program priorities: the Health and Population Sector Strategy (HPSS) in Bangladesh (through task forces on community participation), the Cambodian Health Sector Support Project (through the Ministry of Health Coordination Committee for the project), the Andhra Pradesh First Referral Health System Project and the Uttar Pradesh Health Systems Development Project in India (Murthy and Klugman, 2004, 81), and the Family Health Project (FHP) in Pakistan (Israr and Islam, 2006). In countries of these regions, however, most of the experiences have arisen with the financial aid of foreign donors and international organizations, such as the World Bank – especially relevant at addressing the problem of HIV in West Africa, for instance (Nguyen, 2010). Such institutional origins have been criticized for undercutting national sovereignty, and scholars have suggested unsettling parallels with both colonial rule and post-independence autocracy (Kelly et al., 2017, 1).

[9] In both Europe and Latin America, other experiences of citizens' participation in health exist, such as in Nicaragua, Costa Rica, Mexico, Spain, and Greece. However, these cases were not included because either the information available on these programs is very scant (Nicaragua, Costa Rica, Spain, and Greece) or they are isolated programs that are not translated into legislation (like the program *Aval Ciudadano* in Mexico, or participatory experiences that are not sanctioned by the state).

institution" and "programmatic participation"). After reading those articles, we consulted the relevant cited references that had been published prior to 1998. Finally, we also looked for and analyzed the legal corpus that institutionalizes these participatory experiences: laws, decrees, and public policy programs sanctioned in each country. Our review provided us not only with information about the moments in which programmatic participation in public health was legislated but also the ways in which these institutions were initially regulated and implemented. In the cases of Brazil and Argentina, we also conducted fieldwork. In the case of Brazil, we interviewed local public health authorities and local health councils' members in Porto Alegre and Rio de Janeiro during the summers of 2009 and 2010. In Argentina, we collected archival information on local participatory projects and interviewed key informants in repeated occasions between 2010 and 2018.

3 Programmatic Participation in Health Systems in Western Europe and Latin America

The cross-national comparative analysis of eleven countries (eight in Latin America and three in Western Europe) reveals important differences in the types of health care systems as well as in their processes of reform leading to the inclusion of sectoral participatory institutions. With regard to health care systems, several typologies exist that focus and combine different system variables such as coverage, financing, governance, regulation, ownership of services, and provision and access to services (Blank et al., 2017; Conill et al., 2006; Moran, 1999, 2000; Tuohy, 2003; Wendt et al., 2009). For this Element, we build upon Wendt et al.'s (2009) typology, which distinguishes among health care systems on the bases of (1) financing, (2) health service provision, and (3) regulation. Within each dimension, we analyze the extent to which these activities are led by the state, by societal or non-governmental actors, and/ or by private or market-based actors. In all our country cases, the state monopolizes the regulatory role. Hence, we focus on the dimensions of finance and provision, on which we see variations across cases (see "Health System Features" columns in Table 1).

The comparative cross-country analysis also reveals that in some countries health system overhauls and decentralization reforms were followed by the introduction of participatory institutional mechanisms. Decentralization, to a large extent, was a condition of possibility for citizens' participation in public health. According to Heller (2001, 132), the disenchantment with centralized and bureaucratic states has made the call for decentralization an article of faith: "Strengthening and empowering local government has been justified not only

Table 1 Programmatic Participation in Health Systems in Western Europe and Latin America

	Health System Features				Programmatic Participation Features (*)				
Country	Finance of health services	Provision of health services	Year Health Participation First Legislated	Institutional Origin	Consultation	Monitoring	Planning	Execution	Type of Programmatic Participation
Italy	State	State and private	1978	Health System Overhaul	+	+	-		Monitoring
Portugal	State, societal and private	State and private	1979	Health System Overhaul	+	+	-		Monitoring
Colombia	State and private	State and private	1993	Health System Administrative Decentralization	+	+			Monitoring
Netherlands	Societal	Private	2006	Health System Overhaul	+	+			Monitoring
Cuba	State	State	1961	Social Revolution	+	+	+	+	Policy-making
Brazil	State, societal and private	State and private	1988	Transition to democracy	+	+	+	+	Policy-making
Chile	State, societal and private	State and private	1990	Transition to democracy	+	+	+		Policy-making
Venezuela	State and societal	State and private	1999	Left turn	+	+	+	+	Policy-making
Bolivia	State, societal and private	State and private	2002	Decentralization reform, reoriented by Left turn	+	+	+	+	Policy-making
Ecuador	State, societal and private	State and private	2002	Decentralization reform, reoriented by Left turn	+	+	+		Policy-making
Argentina	State, societal and private	State, societal and private	2006	Left turn	+	+	+	+	Policy-making

Notes: Information on "Health System Features" variables comes from Wendt (2009) and other sources. "Programmatic Participation Features" variables are based on authors' elaboration, as per country case narratives.

(*) Positive (+) and negative (-) signs under civil society participation activities reflect the extent to which those activities are more (+) or less (-) salient in the institutional design.

Figure 1 Programmatic Participation in Health Systems in Western Europe and Latin America since Alma-Ata

on the grounds of making government more efficient but also on the grounds of increasing accountability and participation." The experiences recovered in this volume illustrate that states have created institutions for citizens' participation in health after decentralization reforms. The process of government decentralization in turn has placed more responsibilities, and sometimes resources and authority, in local governments, which thus became significant targets and sites of collective action aimed at affecting the distribution of social services (Falleti, 2005, 2010a).

As with the features of finance and provision of health care services, the institutional designs that promote the participation of citizens in public health are quite varied. As described in the following pages, the comparative analysis shows that different institutional origins lead to varying types of programmatic participation.

Within our cases, the initial adoption of institutional designs to promote citizens' participation in health was embedded in (1) an administrative overhaul of the health system (Italy, Portugal, and the Netherlands); (2) a process of decentralization of government (Colombia, Bolivia, and Ecuador); or (3) a wider political reform process, such as a social revolution (Cuba), a democratic transition (Brazil and Chile), or a left turn in government (Venezuela and Argentina). Table 1 lists countries according to the resulting type of programmatic participation in health (last column), and then chronologically by the first year when participation in health was legislated. The first two columns characterize the health care system, and the remaining columns the features of programmatic participation. Positive and negative signs under civil society's activities reflect the extent to which such features are salient in the institutional design.

Figure 1 represents the countries of our sample along the institutional continuum that goes from the ideal type of programmatic participation for monitoring (with only consultation and monitoring activities) at one end, to the ideal type of programmatic participation for policy making at the other (including the activities of consultation, planning, monitoring, and execution).

In the empirical analysis that follows, we show that if participatory institutions in health were created as part of an administrative health system overhaul, programmatic participation for monitoring prevails. In these cases, the main activities performed by civil society are *consultation* and *monitoring*. These activities can be realized individually, at times even electronically, and do not necessarily require participants to come together with other members of the community. In terms of agenda setting in the participatory institution, we see a more prominent role for the state, which has the last word on what is to be done. At the other end of the spectrum, if participatory institutions were created as part of a political reform process (such as a social revolution, a democratic transition, or a political turn to the left in government*)*, programmatic participation for policy making prevails. Civil society's main activities center on *planning* (including the establishment of priorities) and on the *execution* of programs' activities. These activities presuppose that members of the community come together and work (mostly face-to-face) in a collaborative manner. Civil society tends to have a more prominent role in setting the agenda of participation, and direct mechanisms of participation (unmediated by organizations) are present in these cases.[10] Finally, in those cases where institutions of programmatic participation in health were created in the context of more general decentralization of government policies, the future characteristics of those institutions are tightly linked to the political orientation of future administrations. The two cases that turned to the left (Bolivia and Ecuador) deepened the reforms for community participation and adopted the characteristics of community programmatic participation for policy making, whereas the country that did not (Colombia) remained a case of civic programmatic participation for monitoring.

3.1 Administrative Reforms and Programmatic Participation for Monitoring

The cases of Italy, Portugal, Colombia, and the Netherlands are examples of countries where civic participation in the public health care systems was instituted as part of larger overhauls of their health care systems or sectoral decentralization reform. In these cases, we find that civil society activities center on consultation (or sharing of information) and monitoring, with a secondary (and more recent) role for planning (in the cases of Portugal and Italy). Among these four countries, the first one to significantly reform its health care system and promote community programmatic participation in the sector was Italy, in 1978 – the same year of the Declaration of Alma-Ata. In Portugal, participation in health was first legislated

---

[10] Although with regard to whether recruitment of civil society is direct or indirect, there is no clear emerging pattern related to the institutional origins of participation in health.

in 1979, although it did not start to be regulated until 1990. In Colombia, participation in health was legislated in 1993 and in the Netherlands in 2006 (although patients' organizations had played an important role in consultation since at least the 1990s).

3.1.1 Italy

In Italy, participation of citizens was instituted as part of the broader process of reform of its health care system, which took place first in 1978 and later in the 1990s. In 1978, the National Health Service (*Servizio Sanitario Nazionale*, SSN) was created (Law 833). Italy's SSN was established with the aim of creating an efficient and uniform health care system to cover the entire population, irrespective of income, contributions, employment, or preexisting health conditions, and to promote community control and participation. To date, the SSN provides universal coverage largely free of charge at the point of service to all residents, and emergency care to visitors, irrespective of their nationality.

The 1978 legislative initiative to create the SSN resulted from intense societal pressure, mainly involving trade unions' struggles and social movements' demands (Matos and Serapioni, 2017, 4). At the same time, the public health care reform served the electoral ends of major parties on both the right and left of the political spectrum (Brown, 1984). On the right, the Christian Democrats were worried about cost containment. They were impressed with Britain's experience, where a national health service had made significant strides to make access more equitable at relatively contained costs – many observers at the time found the creation of a national health budget to be the key to the British health system success (Brown, 1984). Thus, Christian Democrats supported the creation of a national health care system. On the left side of the political spectrum, the Communist and Socialist parties were persuaded that the statist and centralist excesses of the past demanded correction by means of decentralization and citizen participation. Hence, Communist and Socialist parties insisted that the SSN be community controlled and promoted the idea of citizen participation (Brown, 1984).

At the heart of the new system were the Local Health Units (*Unità Sanitarie Locali*, USL), complex organizational structures created to absorb the functions of the sickness funds, assume managerial control over public hospitals, and take responsibility for the health needs of geographic areas containing between 50,000 and 100,000 residents. Almost 650 USLs were created at the time of the reform. They were under the authority of the mayor of the municipality, led by a committee of health system users (i.e., consumers staffed the USLs' management councils), and financed with transfers from the central government that set hard budget constraints. The members of the USLs' management councils reflected the balance of power among the political parties in the municipality, as local parties selected the consumer activists who would staff these councils (Brown, 1984, 79–80). The USLs were expected to oversee, organize, and sometimes deliver comprehensive care to local communities (Brown, 1984, 82). But their organizational complexity and the fact that they served several masters (chiefly local parties, the mayor, and the central government) left them highly ineffectual; five years after the reform, participants were still debating the USLs' roles. The USLs increasingly came under attack and would be later transformed.

The 1980s were characterized by jurisdictional conflicts between the different levels of health authorities, since their responsibilities were not clearly delineated, and planning was not consistent between the national and regional levels. Above all, the main problem was the insufficient funding of regional governments, which could not afford the health care needs of their populations. The separation between national funding and regional and local spending was considered the main cause of constantly rising health care expenditures. This, in turn, caused health care to be markedly different in the north and the south of the country, causing concern about the capacity of the health care system to guarantee equal rights to citizens across the country (Ferré et al., 2014, 17).

Hence, since the 1990s, Italy has made significant steps toward federalism, decentralizing political, fiscal, and administrative powers, by means of a major constitutional reform (Baldini and Baldi, 2014). The provision of health has thus been greatly decentralized, with three levels of organization: national, regional, and local. The national level is responsible for ensuring the general objectives and fundamental principles of the SSN. Regional governments, through their regional health departments, are responsible for ensuring the delivery of a package of benefits through a network of population-based local health authorities (*Aziende Sanitarie Locali*, ASLs) and public and private accredited hospitals. At the local level, the SSN is administered by the more than 200 ASLs with approximately 50,000 to 200,000 inhabitants assigned to each. The ASLs, which were created by Legislative Decree 502 of 1992, are a newer version of the previous USLs. Because of managerial problems and an unclear distinction of responsibilities between the national and local levels, the USLs were transformed into the ASLs, which are directly accountable to the regions (Ferré et al., 2014, 20–21). A mixed financing scheme was established that combined general taxation and statutory health insurance contributions, progressively moving to a fully tax-based system (Ferré et al., 2014).

The topic of citizens' participation was reintroduced with Legislative Decree 502 of 1992, which emphasized the *monitoring* function of civic participation.

This decree introduced a quality-control system based on users' assessment of health services (Serapioni and Duxbury, 2014). It also encouraged a *consultation* form of participation, as it promoted the presence, in hospitals and health centers, of associations of volunteers involved in patient care activities, as well as in advisory bodies (Matos and Serapioni, 2017, 4).

Dissatisfaction with the management of health services among different sectors of society, within a context of pronounced decentralization in favor of Italy's regions, prompted the national government to undertake other reforms of the health care system, such as Legislative Decree 229 of 1999. Among other changes, this decree created the regional-level Permanent Conferences for Social and Health Planning, with the purpose of coordinating the participation of representatives of municipalities and local communities (Serapioni and Duxbury, 2014, 491). To date, however, there are few innovative experiences in citizens' participation in the regional health systems in Italy. Among them, one of the most advanced regions is Emília-Romagna, whose Regional Law 19/1994 provides that health centers and hospitals should create adequate conditions for users' associations to conduct advocacy work to propose improvements in the services. This regional law establishes the creation of Mixed Advisory Committees (MAC) consisting of patients and users' representatives, together with health professionals and administrators. MAC participants evaluated the committees positively for their mixed composition, which integrated different cultures, experiences, and professional profiles with the potential to contribute to solving health care problems. However, patients and users' representatives affirmed that in practice, they exerted weak influence on decision making, that their expectations were greater than the results obtained, and that MAC failed to represent some social groups and certain health needs of the population (Serapioni and Duxbury, 2014, 494). Health professionals and administrators ultimately decide whether they will accept patients' and users' associations' recommendations and priorities and patients' associations' experiences, and collaborations are still rarely valued in the health care debate (Goss and Renzi, 2007, 238, 240).

The Italian Ministry of Health reinstated its commitment to fostering different forms of citizen participation in its 2006–2008 National Health Plan, including the direct participation of citizens/patients in decisions regarding treatment and health care and the participation of organizations representing civil society (e.g., patient associations) in determining health care politics (Serapioni and Duxbury, 2014). Despite this new emphasis on participation oriented to making policies, however, citizens have a very limited role and sometimes it is used only to inform or justify decisions taken by others (Goss and Renzi, 2007).

In sum, in Italy, participation includes an active role for citizens in *consultation, monitoring,* and to a lesser extent *planning* of health services at the regional, district, and local levels. The Italian normative framework recognizes the need to provide patients with the appropriate instruments for discussing institutions and services (consultation), and for expressing opinions and evaluations regarding health care services (monitoring) (Goss and Renzi, 2007, 238).

3.1.2 Portugal

During its transition to democracy, the 1976 Constitution institutionalized Portugal as a unitary and decentralized state organized under the principles of subsidiarity, autonomy of local government, and democratic decentralization of public services (Nunes Silva, 2017). The Constitution instituted a new system of local self-government, a subnational system with three tiers – administrative regions, which have not yet been implemented; municipalities; and parishes – all of them with directly elected bodies and with political-administrative and financial autonomy. Since 1976, the competences of the municipalities have expanded. Immediately following the 1974 democratic transition, municipalities' role was heavily focused on infrastructure. Since then, their role in social services has increased (Nunes Silva, 2017, 10). However, in sectors such as education, civil protection, health, social housing, justice, and even road infrastructure, which constitute social obligations of the state, the transfer or delegation of functions to municipalities has been timid and has not led to municipal autonomy in the execution of policies (Nunes Silva, 2017, 14).

With regard to health, Portugal first recognized the right to health in the 1976 Constitution. Under political pressure to reduce large health disparities, the democratic government created the current universal National Health System (*Serviço Nacional de Saúde*, SNS), in 1979, which is comprehensive (full range of services) and "approximately" free of charge (World Health Organization, 2008). The 1979 law establishing the SNS laid down the principles of centralized control with decentralized management. Despite the development of a publicly financed and provided health system, some features of the previous system remain unchanged, namely the health subsystems, which continue to cover a variety of public (civil servants) and private employees (e.g., those in banking and insurance companies, postal service). This law recovers the participatory nature of the national constitution (National Constitution, article 64), and promotes the participation of users of the health system in the planning and evaluation of services (Law 56 of 1979, article 19). The law encourages participation of users in the planning and management of services through the National and Regional Health Councils and the Support Commissions of health centers (Law 56 of 1979, article 23). It also highlights the possibility that users submit individual or collective complaints when services do not guarantee their rights (Law 56 of 1979, article 13). However, it was not until the Health Guidelines Law 35 of 1990 that civic participation in public health would start to be regulated (Crisóstomo et al., 2017, 10).

Following the creation of the SNS, Portuguese health policy went through several reform periods: from the development of an alternative to the public service (in the early 1980s), to the promotion of market mechanisms (in the early to mid-1990s), and the introduction of a number of policies that drifted away from the market-driven health care provision (in the late 1990s). By the beginning of the twenty-first century, the SNS became a mixed system, based on the interaction between the public and the private sectors, integrating primary, secondary, and long-term care. Hence, the Portuguese health system is characterized by three coexisting and overlapping systems: the SNS; the health subsystems, health insurance schemes for which membership is based on professional or occupational group or company; and private voluntary health insurance (Simões et al., 2017).

During the period of promotion of market mechanisms in the early to mid-1990s, there was a split between the state as financer of the health system and the private sector as service providers, who were contracted by the state. In fact, the major role given to the private sector in the supply of care led to discrimination in terms of access to health services and brought the problem of equality to the fore of the public debate once again (Serapioni and Matos, 2014, 228). At this time, the reforms that sought to promote civic participation in health were inspired by the neoliberal principles of New Public Management. The Health Guidelines Law 35 of 1990 and the statute of the National Health Service of 1993 mention consultation type of participation in various areas and levels of the system. On hospital boards, for instance, the consultation committee includes a representative from the users' association. At the primary care level, consultation councils were created to promote public participation (Matos and Serapioni, 2017, 5). As a result of this new institutional framework, patients' associations began to play an important role in participation in health and emerged as new collective actors with increasing visibility (Nunes et al., 2007). They gained an important role in representing and defending patients, which had consequences in subsequent health reforms (Matos and Serapioni, 2017, 5).

More recently, social protest and mobilization against the closure of emergency health centers and maternity wards triggered by the economic crisis (2006–2007), led to Decree 28 of 2008 (Serapioni and Matos, 2014, 228). This decree established the Health Center Groups (*Agrupamentos dos Centros de Saúde*, ACES) with the aim of reducing health inequalities and overcoming the marginalization of primary care. The decree also created Community Councils at the local level to encourage participation by different local actors in decision making and organization of health services. However, in practice, citizens still have scarce opportunities for participation in health (Matos and Serapioni, 2017, 7).

Patients' associations in Portugal have opened up new arenas for debate and proposed alternatives for health governance, as well as health care practices. Within health centers, the community advisory councils give citizens the chance to evaluate the performance of health centers (monitoring) but also to express their opinions on health issues (consultation). Various initiatives have attempted to promote citizens' participation: (1) creation of an observatory in each of the five regional administrations, aimed at improving services and promoting user satisfaction; (2) creation of direct telephone lines between patients and physicians; (3) formalization of procedures for demands and complaints; and (4) creation of advisory councils with users' participation, aimed at supporting the management of health centers and hospitals from the service users' perspective (Matos and Serapioni, 2017, 5). These initiatives underscore the fact that in Portugal, as in the Netherlands and Italy, civic engagement in public health resulted from a larger process of market reform, whereby participants are mostly engaged as consumers, who most importantly evaluate the services and express their opinions, whether individually or in groups (as in the patients' associations and advisory councils). In other words, in Portugal, participation includes an active role of citizens in *consultation* and *monitoring* of health services, but to a lesser extent in the *planning* of them.

3.1.3 Colombia

The Colombian health system is composed of a large social security sector financed with public resources and a shrinking private sector. The affiliation to the system is mandatory and is done through both public and private health-promoting entities (Guerrero et al., 2011). The system is regulated by the Ministry of Health and organized around the General System of Social Security in Health (*Sistema General de Seguridad Social en Salud*, SGSSS).

Participation in health in Colombia followed on the footsteps of a more general process of decentralization of government spanning the 1980s and

1990s, and partially crystalized in the constitutional reform of 1991. During this process, the national health system was also restructured. Health care reform in Colombia was the result of growing social dissatisfaction with the previous system. In a context of crisis of the national State, challenged by internal violence and warfare, both new actors in the field of health (such as prepaid medicine companies) and new social demands (represented in regional and local civic protest movements) emerged (Restrepo et al., 1996). In this context, the health reform of 1993 was the result of heated discussions in Congress, in which the positions of the teams of new technocrats trained in the new economy of health dominated the debate and favored decentralization and community participation in health (Hernández, 2002).[11]

Law 100 of 1993 created the SGSSS, based on competition between health insurers and health service providers and territorial health *councils* as consulting bodies in which territorial entities and actors could participate. The regulatory decree 1,757 of 1994 promoted participation in the organization and control of the system (both direct and indirect), and in 2011, Law 1,438 (article 3), reinforced the supervising role of social participation. Direct participation encompasses the defense of individual rights, based on complaints and claims from users, through the Health Services User Information and Assistance System and the users' service office. Citizens can use telephone lines, suggestion boxes, and customer service offices. Indirect participation entails community participation through their organizations. This type of participation is institutionalized through the Committees for Community Participation (*Comités de Participación Comunitaria* or COPACOs), where user associations and hospital ethics committees focus on the monitoring of health institutions. COPACOs entail municipal-level meetings between the various social actors and the State (Delgado-Gallego and Vázquez-Navarrete, 2006). However, as Mayka (2019) argues, very few COPACOs have been institutionalized and those that exist are very weak.

In conclusion, in Colombia, participation entails both *monitoring* and *consultation*. As Delgado-Gallego and Vázquez-Navarete (2006, 130) argue, participation in health in Colombia is conceived in light of the new political rationality, which organized the provision of health care following the market model and promoted the control of the quality of services by users. Regarding policy decision making, only health personnel and selected social organizations have been included (Noboa et al., 2011). The result is a participatory institution

---

[11] The new economy of health refers to a branch of economics concerned with issues related to efficiency, effectiveness, value, and behavior in the production and consumption of health and health care.

with constrained formal authority, inconsistent implementation, and weak legitimacy (Mayka, 2019).

3.1.4 The Netherlands

Among the group of countries that promoted citizen participation in contexts of management and administrative reforms, the Netherlands is salient as an example of participation in health by relevant health stakeholders. Constitutionally, the Netherlands is a "decentralized unitary state," with a decentralized system of governance (Toonen, 1987). Decentralization reforms started with the neoliberal turn of the 1980s. Former Minister of the Interior and Kingdom Relations Hans Wiegel's 1980 "policy document on decentralization" was the starting point of this wave of reforms (Selnes and Kuindersma, 2006). Since then, decentralization of national policy toward lower-level governments (whether provinces or municipalities) has taken place (Haasnoot, 2012). And since 2015, municipalities have been given greater responsibilities regarding social policies.

Citizen participation in health care was instituted as part of a broader reform of the entire health care system. According to the country's Constitution, the Dutch government is committed to maintaining a health care system that provides access to essential medical care of good quality. For many decades and until 2006, the Netherlands had a compulsory and fragmented system of health insurance for basic medical care that covered a large portion of the Dutch population. Others had to take out private health insurance in which some risk groups were able to obtain a policy offering legally defined, standard coverage. This fragmentation ended in 2006 with the introduction of a single statutory insurance regime that covers all residents of the Netherlands. In this single compulsory insurance scheme, multiple private health insurers compete for insured persons. The state changed its role from direct steering of the system to safeguarding the process from a distance. Responsibilities have been transferred to insurers, providers, and patients. The government only controls the quality, accessibility, and affordability of health care. With regard to financing, all Dutch citizens contribute to this scheme in two ways. First, they pay a flat-rate premium directly to the health insurer of their choice. Second, an income-dependent employer contribution is deducted through their payroll and transferred to the Health Insurance Fund. The resources from this fund are then allocated among the health insurers according to a risk-adjustment system. Finally, in terms of provision, private health care providers are primarily responsible for the provision of health services (Schäfer et al., 2010).

This comprehensive health system reform was the result of years of debate, led by Dutch authorities influenced by the neoliberal turn of the 1980s. A committee chaired by former Philips CEO Wisse Dekker recommended in 1986 the increase of competition among doctors and health insurers, with the primary aim of controlling health costs in the context of an aging population (Haasnoot, 2012). However, due to considerable public opposition, it took until 2005 for the Parliament to pass this reform, which was partially inspired by the Dekker Plan.

The Health Insurance and the Health Care Acts, which came into effect on January 1, 2006, met with broad public consensus. Consumer associations supported this reform, liking the possibility of increased choice and voice for the insured. Conversely, the medical groups, especially general practitioners, opposed the reform, which they saw as a threat to their wages and income (Cohu et al., 2006, 221–223).

Once in effect, the Health Care Act (*Wet marktordening gezondheidszorg*, WMG) began regulating various issues, including the establishment of the Netherlands Health Care Authority (*Nederlandse Zorgautoriteit*, NZa). It defines its tasks, authorities, and instruments, as well as the relationships among the NZa, the Ministry of Health, and other regulators and supervisory authorities (Ministry of Health, Welfare, and Sports, 2011, 14). One of the aims of the WMG is to stimulate social participation of citizens.

At the national level, participation of social actors in the health care system takes place within the National Health Council (*Gezondheidsraad*), which is a statutory advisory body to the government, including the Ministry of Health, Welfare, and Sports. The Council brings together stakeholders and experts on specific topics, on request of the central government or on its own initiative (Den Exter et al., 2004). The Netherlands is an example of participation of citizens through organizations. Lammers (1988, cited by Lamping et al., 2012, 213) characterizes the Dutch health care system as an interorganizational arrangement, that is, a layer of intermediary agencies with representative organizations mandated "from below" and control organizations mandated "from above" interacting.

In the Dutch case, patient organizations are often asked to represent the interests of patients in formal decision making. This model, which can be described as neo-corporatist (Van de Bovenkamp et al., 2010), promotes the interaction of three types of organizations: professional groups, Dutch health insurers, and patient organizations. There is a large number and variety of patient organizations in the Netherlands. Usually, two groups are distinguished: the general organizations that defend the interests of general users of health services and categorical organizations that unite patients with a specific condition or disease (such as diabetes or cancer). Many patient organizations, from both categories, are under the umbrella of the Federation of Patients and Consumer Organizations in the Netherlands (*Nederlandse Patiënten Consumenten Federatie*) founded in 1992 (Schäfer et al., 2010, 31) and a leader in the representation of health care consumers vis-à-vis the government, while disease-specific patient organizations lag behind (Van de Bovenkamp et al., 2010, 83).

At the municipal level, civic participation in health was institutionalized with the Social Support Act (*Wet maatschappelijke ondersteuning*, Wmo), which became law in 2007. According to this Wmo, municipal authorities are responsible for the design and implementation of social support policies for their residents. The guiding principle of the Wmo is participation: municipal authorities have to promote participation of civil society, including those who are deemed vulnerable. The local authority is responsible for these social policies, which have to consider the recipients' needs and their living environment. Hence, municipal authorities have a considerable degree of policy freedom in implementing national social policies at the local level, including those related to civic participation in health.

Most municipal authorities work with a local Wmo council, which includes representatives of various interest groups. Decision making in the Dutch health care system is characterized by *consultation* between the government and stakeholder groups (Ministry of Health, Welfare, and Sports, 2011). Consulting bodies played an important role in this process, and they increased rapidly in number up to 1990. However, as the proliferation of consulting bodies tended to obscure the decision-making process, the Dutch government started reducing their number after the early 1990s (Schäfer et al., 2010). In 2008, the organization of consulting structures to the Ministry of Health, Welfare, and Sports was further revised, resulting in the integration of the Advisory Council of Health Research (*Raad voor Gezondheidsonderzoek*, RGO) into the Health Council (Schäfer et al., 2010, 26).

Although the Dutch health system promotes the participation of citizens in the elaboration of policies, municipal authorities are free to make all necessary arrangements they consider necessary . Hence, although it is advisable to take into account the opinions of citizens and stakeholders, those opinions are not binding. In the context of horizontal accountability, municipal authorities in the Netherlands are also obliged to complete an annual questionnaire on performance and to investigate the degree of satisfaction among social support applicants. This information is published every year before July 1. The municipal authority is also mandated to make these details available to the public. The publication of this data enables the public and civic social organizations to compare the performance of the various municipal governments. Accountability for the policy pursued, hence, is rendered horizontally, not vertically as in other cases of monitoring. In the Netherlands, municipal authorities are held accountable to the local council and the public first, and only secondarily to the national authorities (Ministry of Health Welfare and Sport, 2011, Schäfer et al., 2010). Hence, participation entails the involvement of social organizations related to health both in *consultation* and *monitoring* of the system.

3.2 Political Reforms and Programmatic Participation for Policy Making

In the other seven countries, the adoption of institutions for citizen participation was the result of more general political reform processes, such as social revolution (Cuba), democratic transitions (Brazil and Chile), or the deepening of democracy as part of the Latin American left turn (Venezuela, Argentina, Ecuador, and Bolivia).[12] In these cases, we find that the type of community programmatic participation promoted was oriented more toward policy making and less toward monitoring. As a consequence, the main civil society activities include planning and execution, alongside the activities of consultation and monitoring that we also find in the cases prompted by administrative reforms. In many of these health participatory institutions, civil society sets the collective agenda and in most cases any member of civil society can participate (with or without a mediating organization). The country case narratives that follow are ordered chronologically by the year when participatory institutions in the health sector were first included in legislation.

3.2.1 Cuba

In Cuba, since the 1959 revolution, the State has regulated, financed, and provided health care services. These services operate under the principle that health is an inalienable social right, which defines the Cuban National Health System (*Sistema Nacional de Salud*, SNS) created in 1960 (Law 41). People's health commissions were created in 1961 to implement health policies, and such commissions were key to the future success of the Cuban health system. In these commissions, territorial and social organizations were merely called on to assist health professionals in the delivery of health campaigns – such as

---

[12] It is important to note from the outset that in the case of Venezuela the process of the deepening of democracy ultimately led to its erosion and to Venezuela's downfall into its most profound political and economic crisis, which is having incommensurable humanitarian consequences for Venezuelans, both in the country and abroad.

vaccination campaigns (Feinsilver, 1993, 3), but they did not entail a substantive engagement of local communities in the elaboration or monitoring of policies.

The Cuban SNS is a single health care system, comprehensive, regionalized, and decentralized. It has three administrative levels: national, provincial, and municipal. Responsibilities, spheres of competence, and resources are decentralized to the provincial and municipal levels, guaranteeing local jurisdictions the ability to respond effectively to the demands and needs of each community (Pan-American Health Organization, 2001). The provincial and municipal health directorates are administratively subordinated to the provincial and municipal assemblies, from which they receive their budget, supplies, labor force, and maintenance. Each province forms local health systems in its municipalities (Domínguez-Alonso and Zacea, 2011).

Since Alma-Ata, health decentralization has continued to cement the foundation for social participation in Cuba (Pan-American Health Organization, 2001, Spiegel et al., 2012). After the collapse of the Soviet Union in 1991, Cuba underwent a period of profound economic crisis known as the "special period," which lasted until the late 1990s. At this time, the Cuban government drew from the experiences of the "healthy municipalities" movement (or *Municipios Saludables*), which came together during the International Conference on Health Promotion and Equity in Bogotá, Colombia, in 1992. The Healthy Municipalities movement promoted the idea that local authorities, institutions, public and private organizations, owners, businesspeople, workers, and society in general should devote constant efforts to improve the living conditions, work environments, and culture of the population in a given territory (Sanabria Ramos and Benavides López, 2003, 139–40). Cuba was a pioneer in promoting the Healthy Municipalities movement; in 1995, it created the Network of Healthy Municipalities.

Also in 1995, the National Health Council was created; it consists of the institutions, authorities, organizations, and agencies that intervene in the social production of health. The National Health Council has representations from both provincial and municipal levels. At the local level, social participation has its smallest and most important nuclei in the People's Councils and in the People's Health Councils, "which act as an organ for coordination with certain executive authorities, thus giving concrete expression to the concepts of administrative decentralization and public participation in decision-making and in the government of the country" (Pan-American Health Organization, 2001, 3). These councils must work together with citizens and social organizations (Constitution of Cuba, article 103) and respond mainly to the requests of local citizens and representatives from community organizations (Spiegel et al., 2012).

Thus, programmatic participation in health is defined as one of the main objectives of the health sector in Cuba. To potentiate social participation, health councils exist at all levels of government; they make diagnoses of the health situation, draw action plans, and propose intersectoral solutions in their corresponding localities and territories (Pan-American Health Organization, 2001). At the more local level, People's Health Councils, the most grassroots level of the Cuban government, are in charge not only of monitoring health policies but also planning and executing health programs – for example, health education programs or vaccination campaigns (Keck and Reed, 2012, 17). Furthermore, the inclusion of individuals and representatives from community organizations in local health councils provides a space for broader public involvement and the discussion of other community concerns (Spiegel et al., 2012). This is to say, in Cuba, where civic engagement promotion was the result of the social revolution and the socialist program for health care, participation in health encompasses the four types of civil society activities previously identified: *consultation, planning, monitoring,* and *execution.*

3.2.2 Brazil

During its political transition to democracy, Brazil created a National Single Health System (*Sistema Único de Saúde*, SUS), as part of the new Constitution of 1988 (article 198). In its articles 194 and 198, the Constitution promotes the participation of citizens in the development and execution of social security, which entails the participation of citizens in health issues (Falleti, 2010b; Harris, 2017; Lima et al., 2005). Also, in 1988, the Constitution decentralized SUS services to states and municipalities. In this context, and largely due to the influence of the health sectoral movement of doctors and health practitioners known as the *sanitarista* movement, municipalization of primary health care and citizen participation became cornerstones of SUS (Montekio et al., 2011). The SUS covers 75 percent of the population. Parallel to it, a growing health private sector exists, which includes the Supplementary Medical Care System (*Sistema de Atenção Médica Supletiva*, SAMS) and direct disbursement payments by individuals. (Montekio et al., 2011, 122–123).

The SUS provides services in a decentralized manner through its networks of clinics, hospitals, and other types of federal, state, and municipal facilities, as well as by contracting the services of private establishments, which complement health coverage by public services. The SAMS is a system of insurance schemes that includes group medicine with health plans for companies and families, medical cooperatives, self-administered plans or insurance systems, and individual private plans. The subsystem of direct disbursement is composed of hospitals, clinics, and private laboratories not linked to the SUS, although regulated by the health authorities and used predominantly by the higher-income population (Montekio et al., 2011).

Law 8,080 of 1990 regulates access to and provision of health and establishes that health is a right of all and a duty of the state, guaranteed through social and economic policies aimed at reducing the risk of disease, among other risks. That same year, Law 8,142 created Health Councils (*Conselhos de Saúde*). Health Councils promote the involvement of citizens in health programs and policies. They participate in the formulation and proposition of strategies, the control of the execution of health policies, the decisions on the allocation of resources, the construction of facilities and the implementation of health programs (Moreira and Escorel, 2009, 798). Health Councils also promote citizens' deliberations on health policies and programs and exert social control over the acts of the local authorities destined to implement the decided guidelines (Labra, 2002).

In Brazil, Health Councils exist at every level of government: municipal, state, and federal. In the year 2000, the federal government ruled that each municipal government had to have an operating municipal Health Council as a condition to receive health federal transfers. Thus, practically overnight the number of municipal councils grew significantly and since then practically all of Brazil's 5,500 municipalities have a Health Council. These councils select representatives to the state Health Councils, and those in turn select representatives to the National Health Council, which meets annually in Brazilia and presents a list of policy recommendations to Congress. According to Pogrebinschi (2012), who studied a decade of National Health Councils' meetings and recommendations, approximately half of the National Health Council policy recommendations have been enacted into national law.

At the municipal level, each municipality has its own statute for the formation and selection of members of its municipal council. In all cases, the municipal councils must be formed such that half of their members are users of the public SUS, one-quarter are health practitioners working for the SUS (i.e., doctors and nurses), and one-quarter are administrators of the SUS (public employees of SUS who are not health practitioners) (Labra, 2002, 51). Each municipality decides how to select the representatives of each group. In many municipalities, users are chosen through organizations of civil society that send representatives to the council. Citizens, movements, and/or social associations propose their candidates and vote to select those who will be part of the council. Elections and electoral rules are poorly institutionalized, though. After electing their representatives, citizens and members of the community are also encouraged to participate in the meetings (Coelho Schattan, 2005).

Participation in health in Brazil, then, is instituted through a network of about 5,500 Municipal Health Councils, 27 State Health Councils, and the National Health Council, in which more than 100,000 volunteers participate (Avritzer, 2009; Falleti, 2010b; Moreira and Escorel, 2009). Local and state-level health councils guide the debate on health and the functioning of the SUS based on the National Health Conferences (Montekio et al., 2011; Pogrebinschi, 2013). Civic participation in the public health care system in Brazil thus encompasses the participation activities of *consultation, planning, and monitoring.*

3.2.3 Chile

The Chilean health system consists of two sectors, public and private. The National Health Fund (*Fondo Nacional de Salud*), through the National System of Health Services (*Sistema Nacional de Servicios de Salud*) and its network of Regional Health Services and the Municipal System of Primary Care cover around 70 percent of the national population. The private sector is made up of the Retirement Funds Health Institutions (*Instituciones de Salud Previsional*) and provides services through both private and public facilities. Health is financed by the State, social insurance plans, and also private contributions (Becerril-Montekio et al., 2011). The Chilean Ministry of Health regulates both the public and private sectors.

In Chile, citizen mobilization and participation in health has a long history. Mobilization of the popular classes (urban and rural workers alike) had a central role in the creation and development of the national health system. As Hadjez-Berrios (2014, 91) writes: "the creation of the National Health System in 1952 and its later institutional development until 1973 reflects the historical demands of disadvantaged and marginalized communities, confronted with the antagonist interests of dominant Chilean elites and the Chilean Medical Association." Community Health Councils were created during the administration of Eduardo Frei in the 1960s (Navarro, 1974, 108), and community participation in health continued to advance during the government of Salvador Allende, but the military coup of 1973 aborted such participation. However, those experiences of disadvantaged communities collaborating in health system building and in the social responses to public health problems shaped future participatory practices (Hadjez-Berrios, 2014).

After the return to democracy in 1990, the notion of participatory administration in health was reestablished in a new context of decentralization and a free market economy (Torri, 2012). During that decade, the national government aimed at promoting social participation by creating Participation Committees (*Comités de Participación*) in regional and local health services (Azevedo, 1998, 195). Over the past decade, efforts to create more robust spaces and mechanisms for civic participation transpired in Law 20,500 of 2011 on social participation in the public administration. This law establishes citizens' rights to public information, participatory public administration, civil society strengthening, and nondiscrimination and respect for diversity.

Citizen participation is also supported by the Ministry of Health's norms, guidelines, and performance incentives. The Ministry of Health defines community participation in health as a process of cooperation in which the state and citizens jointly identify problems and deliberate on their solutions, with methodologies and tools that promote reflection and collective dialogue (Frenz et al., 2017, 5). Community participation in health is related then to civil society's capacity to influence public health decisions. Civil society's input ranges from the design, implementation, and evaluation of policies, plans, programs, and projects linked to recovery, rehabilitation, and prevention of disease and health promotion to decisions related to the use and investment of public resources (Ministerio de Salud, 2015, 1, cited in Frenz et al., 2017, 6).

Hence, in Chile, participation entails the engagement of citizens in the activities of *consultation, monitoring*, and *planning*. Civil society and citizen councils are the formal participatory bodies with consulting, control, and increasingly deliberative roles, which are an integral part of the public health system's institutional and management framework at all levels (Artaza-Barrios et al., 2013). However, as Delamaza and Ochsenius (2010) highlight, whereas citizens' participation in public health has been promoted in the recent past, the less organized sectors of civil society exert less influence on the policy-making process than the more organized groups, such as health care providers. Similarly, other authors argue that civic participation in health is linked to the needs of health facilities and has a passive and supervised modality in response to institutional guidelines (Cooke and Kothari, 2001; Jara and Torres Andrade, 2015). This problem is at times compounded by lack or difficulty of accessing information, which also discourages the effective participation of citizens.

3.2.4 Venezuela

Although civic participation in health had been an aspiration of the process of administrative decentralization initiated in Venezuela in the late 1980s (for a detailed account of this process of decentralization reform in the 1990s, see

Grindle, 2000, chapter 4), it was only adopted with the ascension of Hugo Chavez to government in 1999. As soon as he took office, Chavez called for a Constituent Assembly, in which the issue of health took on great importance. During the constituent process, several social organizations participated to influence the final result of the Constitution. Among them, the participation of actors such as the National Coordinator of Community Participation in Health and the local health committees that existed de facto in several states of the country were extremely salient (Uzcategui, 2012). Cuban doctors also participated in the constituent process, and their experiences were a crucial input in the final content of the Constitution and the subsequent laws on health participation (Uzcategui, 2012). The Constitution of 1999, thus, recognizes health as an integral social right, guaranteed as part of the right to life and a dignified level of welfare.

The Organic Health Law (*Ley Orgánica de Salud de la República Bolivariana de Venezuela*) of 1998 organizes the health sector, but the health system has been in a process of change since 1999. Since then, the Ministry of Health has proposed a model of comprehensive care for the population and the creation of a National Public Health System (*Sistema Público Nacional de Salud*, SPNS) with the aim of guaranteeing the right to health of all Venezuelans. The SPNS was defined as intergovernmental, decentralized, and participatory (which implies that national policies, plans, and actions must be coordinated with the State and municipal governments, promoting the decentralization of the sector and citizen participation). However, the SPNS creation process has been slow and has not yet been finalized. In practice, the structure of the traditional Venezuelan health system, highly fragmented in a set of subsystems unequally organized and without universal access to health services, has been maintained. The Ministry of Health regulates the public sector, where a network of hospitals and outpatient services of the subnational states – which have been severely and negatively affected by the economic crisis starting in 2014 – provides services. The private sector is made up of service providers and health insurance companies, which offer assistance from the most basic to the most specialized in exchange for direct payments. The health system is financed mainly with money from the State and contributions from workers (Armada et al., 2009; Bonvecchio et al., 2011).

The health care reform program of the 1999 Constitution was first formalized around 2003 and 2004 with the program *Misión Barrio Adentro*, which had a participatory component (for an excellent description of the origins of the program, see Armada et al., 2009). At the primary level, the health care model of *Barrio Adentro* had a small catchment area (between 250 and 400 families), mandated the health professionals of community health centers to do home visits as well as visits to schools and workplaces, and had a participatory model: the design and realization of all activities were to be controlled by decisions taken by the community, with residents of the catchment neighborhood participating in administration and delivery of primary health care (Armada et al., 2009, 168). The program also had a training component, forming community health promoters (another way in which the community participated programmatically in the health sector). This is to say, in the language of our typology of civil society's participation activities, the program entailed consultation, planning, and execution by civil society.

Barrio Adentro was highly informed by the Cuban experience in public health and primary care. In fact, 75 percent of the total number of doctors, nurses, and dentists employed by this program in 2005 (26,500 employees in total) were of Cuban origin. But this led to disagreement from the Venezuelan opposition, which saw the program as undermining Venezuela's sovereignty, and from the Federation of Venezuelan Doctors (*Federación Médica de Venezuela*), which considered the program to be of poor quality and blocked referrals from the program at the secondary and tertiary levels of health services.

Despite the opposition, between 2003 and 2006 the number of local health committees (*Comités de Salud*) in the *Barrio Adentro* program increased from just over 2,000 to almost 9,000 (Armada et al., 2009, 169), hence significantly extending primary care coverage in Venezuela.[13] Yet, the fragmentation in funding, even within the public system, as well as the lack of coordination and collaboration among the primary, secondary, tertiary, and quaternary levels of health care services, compounded with the economic crisis, has led to the abandonment of the program and the return of the Cuban doctors to their home country.

Besides the program *Barrio Adentro*, during the period of the Bolivarian Revolution and in the legal system, various laws and regulatory instruments have laid the legal foundations for civic participation, including in health (Sáez González, 2015, 135).[14] In particular, the laws of Communal Councils define these local institutions as the main instances of participation, articulation, and integration among citizens, the various community organizations, and social and popular movements. These participatory institutions were an attempt to

---

[13] According to Armada et al. (2009, 171), *Barrio Adentro* reached 17 million Venezuelans by 2005.

[14] These are, among others, the Constitution of the Bolivarian Republic of Venezuela of 1999; the Communal Councils Law of 2006; Organic Law of the Communal Councils of 2009; and of 2010: the Organic Law of the People's Power, the Organic Law of the Municipal Public Power, the Law of the Local Councils of Public Planning, the Organic Law of Popular Public Planning, and the Organic Law of the Communes.

respond to the needs of historically excluded local populations and were conceived as an alternative to the representative model of articulation of citizens through political parties (Ellner, 2008; Zaremberg, 2012).

As in Cuba, the Venezuelan Communal Councils were meant as tools of direct or radical democracy. The councils were supposed to allow organized citizens to exercise the full government of the community and to directly manage public policies and projects aiming to respond to the needs, possibilities, and aspirations of the communities (Law of the Communal Councils of 2009, article 2). This participatory philosophy extends to the health committees that are embedded in the communal councils. Each Communal Council was designed to have an "executive organ" that implements all the decisions voted by the Assembly of Citizens and its working committees (including health). Each Communal Council also had a monitoring unit in charge of evaluating the execution of programs and expenditures (Teruggi, 2012, 50).[15]

As implemented through the communal councils, participation in health was meant to encompass the four types of civil society participation activities: *consultation, planning, monitoring*, and *execution*. However, the extent to which the health committees did in fact develop these activities remains contested (Lupien, 2018; Zaremberg, 2012). For instance, citizens affirm that they can participate in Communal Councils, but their efficacy is limited because those in charge of leading the discussions do not listen to their opinions, or just because Councils cannot reach a successful policy to solve local problems (Fundación Centro Gumilla, 2009).

3.2.5 Bolivia

Bolivia has a public and a private health sector. The public sector includes the Ministry of Health and Sports (*Ministerio de Salud y Deportes*, MSD) and the social subsector. The social subsector comprises the health funds (*Cajas de Salud*), university insurances, and the General Directorate of Health. The private sector is made up of insurance companies and private and nonprofit health service providers. The MSD has the responsibility of regulating the overall health care system. Health is financed by the State, social insurance plans (*Cajas de Salud*), and also private contributions (Ledo and Soria, 2011).

---

[15] All citizens can participate in their Communal Council by the Assembly of Citizens, which is composed of the inhabitants of the community who are at least fifteen years old. Decisions, which are made by the direct vote of citizens, are binding for the respective Communal Council. In this context, citizens can be part of and vote in the working committees, including the health committee (Hanson, 2018, 150; Teruggi, 2012).

In Bolivia, decentralization and civic participation in health had their origins in the 1990s. Together with privatization and education reform, decentralization of government was one of the three main reform pillars of the first presidency of Gonzalo Sánchez de Losada (1993–1997), leader of the National Revolutionary Movement Party (*Movimiento Nacional Revolucionario*, MNR).[16] The decentralization program was enacted in the Popular Participation Law of 1994 (*Ley de Participación Popular*, LPP) (Davies and Falleti, 2017; Faguet, 2012; Galindo and Medina, 1995). As stated in its preamble, the main goal of this law was to improve citizens' quality of life by perfecting representative democracy and facilitating participation (Faguet, 2014, 3). The law, in its first article, "recognizes, promotes and consolidates the process of Popular Participation, articulating the indigenous, peasant and urban communities in the legal, political and economic life of the country." This law significantly changed the Bolivian intergovernmental and local institutional landscape. The LPP decentralized fiscal and political power from the national government to the municipalities, redrew the Bolivian map by almost tripling the number of municipalities – from 117 to 315 at the time – and designed an institutional framework at the municipal level for civic participation and the oversight of local authorities. The LPP assigned 20 percent of national tax revenues to municipal governments along with responsibility for maintenance and construction of schools, health clinics, secondary roads, micro-irrigation systems, and sports facilities (Kohl, 2003, 156).[17]

The LPP created an institutional framework for participatory planning by neighborhood and indigenous organizations. It recognized community-based organizations, which included urban neighborhood organizations, indigenous organizations, and peasant unions. Thanks to this law, in only three years (between 1994 and 1997) the government registered almost 15,000 grassroots territorial organizations. At the municipal level, these organizations were charged with the responsibility of crafting annual operating plans and five-year municipal development plans, overseeing projects, and mobilizing community labor for the construction and maintenance of public works (Kohl, 2003, 156). The law also created oversight committees with members drawn from the community, with the power to veto municipal budgets and recall mayors.[18] Also during the presidency of

---

[16] Interview with Alfonso García, National Director of Municipal Empowering in the National Secretary of Popular Participation between 1994 and 1997. Interview carried out in Quito, Ecuador, June 12, 2013.

[17] Prior to the LPP, three cities (La Paz, Cochabamba, and Santa Cruz) captured 93 percent of the total national funding directed to municipalities (Kohl, 2003, 156).

[18] See Hiskey and Seligson (2003) for a critical assessment of the political impact of the oversight committees.

Sánchez de Losada, Law 2,426 of 2002 of universal insurance for mothers and infants created the Local Health Directories (*Directorios Locales de Salud*, DILOS), instances of citizen participation and social control in the public health sector (Galindo, 2016).

Since Evo Morales ascended to the presidency in 2006, the Bolivian government has passed a number of laws aimed at developing new modes of citizen participation. In Bolivia, policy makers under the socialist government of Morales recovered the main postulates of the Declaration of Alma-Ata, regarding primary health care and participation in health (Silva et al., 2009). In particular, to improve health indicators the Bolivian government (and also the Ecuadorian government under Correa) based its new policies on the main postulates of the Latin-American Social Medicine Association (*Asociación Latinoamericana de Medicina Social*, ALAMES), which proposes an approach based on the participation of communities (Silva et al., 2009).

Civic participation in health has been institutionalized in the Constitution of 2009, which states that citizen participation and social control are political rights. In its article 40, it also establishes that the state will guarantee the participation of the organized population in decision making, and in the management of the entire public health system. The health system is rather unique, defined as universal, free, equitable, intra-cultural, intercultural, participatory, with quality, and social control (Constitution of 2009, article 19). The system is based on the principles of solidarity, efficiency, and coresponsibility, and it is developed through public policies at all levels of government.

Moreover, Law 31 on Autonomies and Decentralization of 2010 and Law 341 on Participation and Social Control of 2013 state that participation in health relates to *consultation, planning, monitoring*, and *execution* of health policies. To do so, citizens participate in Health Municipal Councils (*Consejo Social Municipal de Salud,* COMUSA), new incarnations of the DILOS. The Health Municipal Councils work together with the local civil society to prepare a Municipal Health Plan that is included in the Municipal Development Plan. They prioritize programs by using citizens' and social organization's demands (Galindo, 2016, 82). After the programs are decided, not only members of the Councils but also members of the community have the duty of executing them (Ministerio de Salud de Bolivia, 2015).

3.2.6 Ecuador

Ecuador, like many unitary countries, has a marked centralist tradition that historically has concentrated the weight of the State administration and the responsibilities of government at the central level. Even demographically, Ecuador shows a high population concentration in the cities of Quito and Guayaquil.

The process of decentralization that began in the 1990s had timid beginnings, targeting mainly the local level, and did not propose an integral system of political and administrative reform of the State (Serrano and Acosta, 2011). The adoption of decentralizing legislation can be traced to the advocacy of liberalizing presidents like Jamil Manhuad (1998–2000) and to pro-market parties like the Social Christian Party that used its cabinet influence to demand decentralization (Eaton, 2014, 1134). In 1997, almost two decades after the return to democracy, Congress passed the so-called Law of 15%.[19] According to this law, the central government had to transfer 15 percent of its income to subnational governments. Soon thereafter, it passed Law 27 of Decentralization of the State and Social Participation, which advocated for the funded decentralization of responsibilities such as health, education, housing, and environmental protection, among others, to municipalities.[20] The Constitution of 1998 continued to build the legal framework to decentralize government. Its brief Title XI was dedicated to decentralization and territorial organization. It established that no administrative decentralization could take place without the supporting fiscal decentralization, and vice versa. It also stated that subnational units could request decentralization of responsibilities, such as health or education.

In 2002, the Congress passed the Organic Law of the National Health System (*Ley Orgánica del Sistema Nacional de Salud*, LOSNS), which established the legal framework for the organization of the health system, as established in the 1998 constitution. The health system of Ecuador is composed of two sectors: public and private. The public sector includes the Ministry of Public Health (*Ministerio de Salud Pública*, MSP), the health services of municipalities, and the social security institutions. The MSP offers health care services to the entire population and is responsible for regulating health policies in the country. The private sector includes for-profit institutions (hospitals, clinics, dispensaries, pharmacies, and prepaid medicine companies) and nonprofit

---

[19] *Ley Especial de Distribución del 15% del Presupuesto del Gobierno Central para los Gobiernos Seccionales*. Besides establishing the 15 percent transfer to subnational governments, this law stated that municipalities would receive 70 percent of these transfers and provinces would receive 30 percent (Faust and Harbers, 2011, 72).

[20] See Law 27, *Ley Especial de Descentralización del Estado y de Participacion Social*.

organizations of civil society. Health is financed by the State, social insurance plans, and private contributions (Lucio et al., 2011).

From 2002 onward, a process that promotes the participatory and consensual construction of the National Health System has been initiated, based on the structuring of the Provincial and Cantonal Health Councils, whose constitution and functioning represent the consolidation and strengthening of the national health system, as indicated in the LOSNS (Ministry of Health of Ecuador, 2007). Although the participation of citizens in the scope of health was first mentioned in the LOSNS, it was the government of President Rafael Correa (2007–2017) that implemented these institutions. In 2009, the Congress on Health and Life (*Congreso por la Salud y por la Vida*, COSAVI) focused on the issue of social participation.[21] After this COSAVI, the government decided to stop them[22] but instituted other forms of participation. In 2010, the Organic Law on Citizen's Participation (article 52) created the Citizen Council on Health, which acts as a civil society participation network articulated with the national health authority. At the local level, the law created assemblies by which citizens can participate (either individually or collectively) in the proposal and monitoring of health policies, among other activities. Up to 2015, the government had created 1,843 of these councils.[23]

Thus, although decentralization has been timid in Ecuador, participation in health entails to some degree (and at least in the legislation) *consultation, planning*, and *monitoring* (Organic Law on Citizen's Participation, articles 60, 61, and 62). The local assemblies elect the members of local health committees, which are formed by citizens and social organizations (Carvajal, 2016). Each local health committee is in charge of identifying health priorities,

---

[21] The COSAVIs were created by the Organic Law of the National Health System in 2002. They are instances in which health professionals, the State, and social organizations join together to discuss health policies (Noboa et al., 2011, 27). COSAVIs were held in 2002, 2004, 2007, and 2009. Before 2009, COSAVIs also promoted the participation of social actors. For instance, the II COSAVI (in 2004) had "801 participants." It (also) must be stressed that the meeting achieved a greater participation of civil society delegates, among which representatives of women's movements, youth, indigenous organizations, neighborhood federations, NGOs, and trade associations stood out. Together with the representatives of public and private health sector institutions, these actors contributed to the enrichment of the debate and the formulation of proposals for the political agenda of the II Congress. (www.conasa.gob.ec/index.php? option=com_content&view=article&id=143&Itemid=164)

[22] In 2016, different social organizations organized the V COSAVI, which was labeled "Health in Resistance" (*La Salud en Resistencia*). In the meeting, participants denounced that Correa was not applying the LOSNS and that citizen participation was centralized and managed by the central government (https://issuu.com/matiascuvi/docs/memorias_cosavi_baja).

[23] *El Comercio*, October 15, 2015, www.elcomercio.com/tendencias/escuelas-participacionciudadana-carinavance-guayas-ministeriodesalud.html

planning local health plans with health authorities, and monitoring the execution of the plan.

3.2.7 Argentina

During the twentieth century, Argentina's health system evolved into a fragmented system with three subsystems: the public sector, which offers free health services through its network of hospitals and primary care health clinics; the social insurance sector of the so-called *obras sociales*, for the formal workers of the economy and retirees; and the private health insurance sector. In 2010, according to the National Statistics and Censuses Institute of Argentina (*Instituto Nacional de Estadística y Censos*, INDEC), 38.4 percent of the population was covered exclusively by the public system, 46 percent by *obras sociales*, and the remaining 15.6 percent by the private health sector.

In the public health sector, decentralization of national health services toward the provinces took place in 1978, in the context of the last military dictatorship.[24] By Law 21,883 of that year, the national government transferred sixty-five hospitals to provinces and municipalities (Cetrángolo and Jiménez, 2003, 53, n. 69). The process continued in 1991, during the period of neoliberal economic reforms commanded by President Carlos Menem (1989–1995, 1995–1999) and his minister of economy, Domingo Cavallo (for a description of this process, see among others, Eaton, 2002, 2004; Falleti, 2010a, chapter 3; Tobar, 2006, 80; 2012, 12).

At the time of the conference of Alma-Ata, in 1978, Argentina was in the second year of its most violent and repressive military dictatorship. As the military government was offloading health services onto subnational governments, it also adopted the label of Primary Health Care (*Atención Primaria de la Salud*, APS) to refer to the territorially based programs of health care, sanitation, and disease prevention that had been in operation since the 1960s. These programs had developed in rural areas, particularly in the northwestern provinces of Jujuy, Salta, and Tucumán (around the production of sugar, cotton, and tobacco), in the province of Neuquén, and in the suburban and poor peripheries of large urban centers, such as Buenos Aires. Other than creating the APS label to refer to these primary health care programs, the military government actively discouraged community participation. In fact, the authoritarian regime considered the activities related to promotion of community participation in health care to be "subversive," and hence subject

---

[24] According to Acuña and Chudnovsky (2002, 9), this was the fourth stage in the process of evolution of the Argentine health system, which they name "fiscal decentralization" of the system. It came after the stages of anarchic decentralization (up to 1945), centralization (1945–1955), and system decentralization (1955–1978).

to its systematic state repression. A health agent working at the time in the department of Güemes, in the northern province of Salta, expressed this state of affairs very eloquently: "in 1978, Primary Health Care is born ... with one condition: without community participation. It was very clear. We could do anything we wanted, but without participation. 'Come on, please [it was said at the time] you shall not promote subversion'" (cited in Berlotto et al., 2012, 368, our translation).

With the transition to democracy in 1983, some social programs directed to vulnerable populations began to promote community participation. However, they remained highly localized and outside the purview of the Ministry of Health. In fact, toward the end of the first democratic transition government of President Raúl Alfonsín (1983–1989), the idea that community participation in health was part of a leftist and subversive political agenda was still deeply rooted in some sectors of society, and in particular among the federal and provincial security forces. As Dr. Carlos Anigstein, a pediatrician and primary care doctor, who worked on APS at the time, told us:

> Although it may be hard to believe, when I was in the hospital [Ramón Carrillo, in the province of Buenos Aires], two car bombs were placed in my car and I received death threats. I have a Jewish surname ... 'We are going to kill you, *judío de mierda.*' But then, when the federal police came and when the security intelligence services came, they would tell me 'What do you expect, Doctor? Considering the work you do ... ' For them, anything having to do with participation was subversive ... Even though we were in 1989 [six years into the democratic government].[25]

It was only after the 2001 economic and political crisis that community participation in health entered the national government's agenda, largely as a way to address the immediate post-crisis health care needs of the most vulnerable social sectors. Community participation in monitoring (first) and planning (later) of health programs and projects was also inspired by the inclusionary ideology of policy designers who became policy makers at the federal level. Some of these policy makers had been working in primary health care since the early 1970s and had been deeply influenced by the participatory experiences of Cuba (in the 1960s) and Brazil (since the late 1980s).

During the administration of Dr. Ginés González García as national minister of health and the environment (2002–2007), these now national-level policy makers promoted community participation in a federal network of primary and preventive health care programs. Among the policy makers who designed

---

[25] Interview with Carlos Anigstein, pediatrician and founder of REMEDIAR program, in Buenos Aires, December 28, 2017.

participatory policies were Dr. Carlos Pacheco, Dr. Carlos Anigstein, and sociologist Federico Tobar. These national-level programs included, among others, the program *REMEDIAR* (2002–2017), the program Community Doctors (*Médicos Comunitarios*),[26] the program Healthy Municipalities (*Municipalidades Saludables*), and the program Local Participatory Projects (*Proyectos Locales Participativos*, PLPs), which we analyze.

REMEDIAR, a program for the distribution of free medicines through the public primary health care clinics (*Centros de Asistencia Primaria de la Salud*, CAPS), was the stewardship program.[27] It was designed to address some of the most dire needs of the population after the 2001 economic crisis.[28] It consisted of the delivery of commonly prescribed and generic drugs for patients of the CAPS, throughout the Argentine territory. By 2006, the program distributed boxes of generic drugs (*botiquines*) to approximately 5,000 CAPS throughout the country (Tobar, 2006). In 2007, its fifth anniversary, the program produced a descriptive video: *Remediar 5 Años*. By the year 2012 (when the program was in its tenth year running), President Cristina Fernandez de Kirchner (2007–2015) distributed the *botiquin* number 1,500,000 (Redes, 2012). In the national offices of the Ministry of Health, REMEDIAR was run by a relatively small and highly trained group of young professionals. They were mindful about social needs and inequities in the distribution of public health benefits and sought to address issues of efficiency in public spending (through bulk purchase of generic drugs, for instance) and in the delivery of these drugs to patients, such that the medicines (or *botiquines*) would reach the CAPS and their patients. To curb possible deviation of these resources, civil society organizations were invited to participate as monitors of the program.

---

[26] This is a national-level program of community health agents (including social workers) running since approximately 2009. The health agents are paid "fellowships" (or becas) by the National Ministry of Health and are primarily in charge of doing house visits in poor neighborhoods. By 2015, agents were denouncing the national government for lack of payment (www.change .org/p/ministerio-de-salud-de-la-nacion-programa-medicos-comunitarios-programa-nacional-medicos-comunitarios-programa-nacional-de-medicos-comunitarios-necesitamos-cobrar-nuestros-sueldos-urgente). Since 2017 there have been attempts at ending the program and provincial authorities complain that they are not receiving the national transfers to pay for the program (www.cadena3.com/contenido/2017/07/10/Reclaman-fondos-de-la-Nacion-para-Medicos-Comunitarios-187460.asp).

[27] CAPS are the primary health care clinics of the public health system in Argentina. There are more than 7,500 CAPS in Argentina – in urban areas, some CAPS operate within hospitals. In general, CAPS are the first trenches of the public health system and in charge of vaccination campaigns and health programs for pregnant women and babies.

[28] As a direct consequence of the economic crisis of 2001, 50 percent of the population lived under poverty and 27.5 percent under extreme poverty in Argentina in 2002.

As a health care program, REMEDIAR is particularly salient for several reasons. First, it was (to our knowledge) the first national level program to promote civic engagement in health policies. The program had ten explicit goals; among them were strengthening of primary health care, direct distribution of medicines, direct social control, participation, and transparency (Redes, 2012, 21–22). Even if at the beginning of the program, civil society engagement was limited to the role of monitoring (society as watchdogs of local officials that the central government could not fully monitor), such participation extended over time to other types, involving planning and execution, as we explain later. Second, REMEDIAR is important because it was the longest-running program among those that fomented participation, surviving through several presidential administrations (from Eduardo Duhalde to Néstor Kirchner and Cristina Fernández de Kirchner).[29] Third, it fostered the implementation of other participatory programs, such as the Local Participatory Projects (PLPs), which we analyze in the fourth section of this Element.

As mentioned, civic community involvement in the program REMEDIAR was primarily monitoring. Civil society organizations and individuals worked as "watchdogs" that the nationally provided *botiquines* were reaching the CAPS' patients and not being diverted to other uses or being distributed by political personnel in exchange for political support. This type of community monitoring was described as "social direct control."[30] The ministry worked with Caritas (a Catholic organization) and the Red Cross (a nonreligious institution) both at the central level and in the localities.[31]

Closely related to REMEDIAR, the Local Participatory Projects (*Proyectos Locales Participativos*, PLPs) program sought to augment civic participation in health, not only in the monitoring role of participation but also in planning (*planificación participativa*) and execution. The program's

---

[29] After fifteen years in operation, REMEDIAR was ended by President Mauricio Macri (2015–present). In lieu of this program, some medicines are distributed to the CAPS under the Universal Coverage Program (*Cobertura Universal de Salud*, CUS), created in 2016. However, as eloquently put by a CAPS director in the northern province of Formosa: "Before, when the REMEDIAR box arrived, the box was heavy, you needed two people to lift it. Now, when the new box of medicines arrives, you can lift it with two fingers, and you shake it and there are two things inside and it sounds like a baby rattle." Interview with Julio César Scalora, pediatrician and director of CAPS 6343, La Primavera, Formosa, on July 31, 2018.

[30] Interviews with Andrea Casabal, social worker, founder of Local Participatory Projects, Ministry of Health and the Environment, July 16, 2009, Buenos Aires; and with Lic. Mauricio Monsalvo, REMEDIAR Program, Ministry of Health and the Environment, July 16, 2009, Buenos Aires.

[31] These two NGOs would later be directly involved in the evaluation of PLP projects, both at the stage of selection of projects for funding (at the national level), as well as in the evaluation of how the projects were evolving midway through the year of funding (in the localities).

origins are found in 2004, when the area dedicated to participation of the REMEDIAR program put out a call for community narratives of health (or *Relatos*) from the CAPS.[32]

As the narratives started to pour in to the central offices of the National Health Ministry, the personnel who read the narratives realized that many of them (whether in the form of letters, short stories, or photo compositions) were in fact presenting projects to work with the community or to improve the CAPS.[33] In fact, the narratives were so many and so interesting that the personnel of the Ministry of Health gave awards to some in a national event. It was then that the idea of putting out a call for community participation proposals through the CAPS started to take shape. Such an idea found fertile institutional ground in that those leading the ministry liked it and were willing to support it. This is to say, political support for this project at the leadership level in the Ministry of Health was fundamental to the project being born. Such support, or lack thereof, also explained the future instability of the program.

Programmatic participation in the local participatory projects in Argentina involved the activities of *consultation, planning, monitoring,* and *execution*. The recruitment of participants was open to all members of society in the catchment of the CAPSs. However, designed and implemented from above, this participatory program would lose funding and

---

[32] At the back of the newsletter of the REMEDIAR program, a highlighted announcement read as follows:

Hi ...

Today we want to start a new type of dialogue with you, the quiet and many times silenced protagonists of the Health Care System: the CAPS workers, without distinctions of professions, specialties, or functions.

We want to recover – from the point of view of your concerns – the everyday know-hows. Those know-hows that most times have been ignored, because in very few opportunities (or ever) anyone has cared to ask you.

We want you to tell us about the obstacles [you have found], how did you confront them, about your frustrations, your achievements, and the shadows.

We want to listen to the opinions of the doctors who were trained [to address] illnesses.

We want to listen to the opinions of nurses, administrators, housekeepers, sanitary agents. We need to listen to the social workers, please tell us your opinions.

We will only seek to facilitate that your voices will be heard, but first and foremost, we will try to listen ourselves first.

Health is a road [camino] to build, it is a permanent "way of being" [estar siendo], and in that being, you and your opinions are indispensable [insustituibles]. PROAPS – REMEDIAR – Area de Participation. [followed by an email address]. (Boletín PROAPS-REMEDIAR, Atención Primaria de la Salud, Vol. 2, Nr. 12, July 2004, p. 24, our translation)

[33] Interview with Andrea Casabal, August 1, 2017, Buenos Aires.

support with a change in the leadership of the Ministry of Health and would be abandoned with the turn to the right in the Argentine national-level government after 2015.

4 Community Programmatic Participation for Policy Making: The Case of Participatory Local Projects in Argentina

In this section, we analyze an example of programmatic participation in health that involves the civil society activity of *execution*. We chose this program largely for practical reasons: we were allowed access and able to compile a large amount of primary data on it. With this program, Argentina is, together with Cuba, Bolivia, and Venezuela, one of the four countries in the eleven-country sample of cases with programmatic participation in health that includes the civil society activity of *execution*. We analyze the second national call for Local Participatory Projects (*Programas Locales Participativos*, PLPs). These projects were launched in July 2007 and ran until mid-to-late 2008.

After the CAPS' narratives described in the previous section poured in the offices of the National Ministry of Health, the first national call for PLPs' proposals took place in 2006. At the national level, the PLPs program was led by three social workers highly committed to the ideas of community participation and civic engagement.[34] They worked in close collaboration with the REMEDIAR program, which already had expertise with thousands of primary health care centers (*Centros de Atención Primaria de la Salud*, CAPS) throughout the country. Three hundred and sixty-nine projects were presented to the ministry that year. With funding from an international loan, 198 projects were selected and financed.[35] The projects were distributed throughout 23 of the provinces and the City of Buenos Aires (only the most southern province of Tierra del Fuego did not have a participatory project that year).

The 2006 call for proposals had a carefully crafted series of guidelines about community participatory planning, specifically on how to prioritize health and sanitation problems to be tackled by the community. The problem prioritization model was one of the steps of the guidelines and it is worth describing, as these

---

[34] These were Andrea Casabal (the only member of the team who was still working in the National Ministry after 2011), Cristina Ruano, and Daniel Ventura. We are thankful to them for answering all our questions over several interviews and for helping us navigate the PLPs' information.

[35] We do not have information on how the project selection took place in the first PLP call for proposals in 2006.

problems are excellent descriptors of the socioeconomic context of the communities carrying out the PLPs. For each problem that the community identified, six questions had to be asked and the answers scored between 0 and 4: (1) How many in the population of this social group are affected by this problem? (most=4; half=3; less than half=2; few=1; very few=0); (2) What is the expected trend for the upcoming years? (increasing=4; slightly increasing=3; unstable=2; stable=1; decreasing=0); (3) What is the likelihood that this problem will generate important harm? (very high=4; high=3; medium=2; low=1; none=0); (4) What is the likelihood that preventive actions will reduce this harm? (very high=4; high=3; medium=2; low=1, none=0); (5) What are the type of solutions that exist: Institutionally? (very high=4; high=3; medium=2; low=1, none=0), Financially? (low cost=4; medium cost=3; high cost=2; very high cost=1; there are no resources=0), and Communally? (very high=4; high=3; medium=2; low=1, none=0); (6) What is the community's degree of interest in solving the problem? (very high=4; high=3; medium=2; low=1, none=0).

Thus, in a meeting with the CAPS' health agents, the members of civil society gathered to identify the most pressing problems in their communities and rank them according to these criteria. The use of boards or posters was encouraged to track the problems and questions' scores (for the illiterate population, these problems were represented by hand-drawn images). The communities were also encouraged to brainstorm on boards and posters the root causes of the problems identified and distinguish among those that could be addressed with community involvement through this program and those that were not addressable. For example, while the lack of receptacles to dispose of trash was an addressable cause, the inadequate service of trash collection in the locality was not.

The national ministry team produced a video entitled "Protagonistas" with interviews of health agents and community members of seven of these projects in five Argentine provinces. The first project presented in the video, from the CAPS Las Pircas, in the municipality of La Merced, Salta, depicts the use of posters and drawings to identify problems (presumably because at least part of the population of the CAPS catchment is illiterate), prioritize them following the guidelines, and brainstorm about the addressable causes of those problems. In that community, the prioritized problem was water treatment (the project was entitled Water and Life, or *Agua y Vida*).

All the seven cases recorded in the video portray participant communities that are poor or extremely poor. In the case of the community project in Godoy Cruz, Mendoza, for instance, all the members of the community live off scavenging in a nearby dumping site. In the northern community of Rosario de Lerma, Salta, the participants in the project are mostly indigenous, and the communal project consisted of a vegetable garden. As a community member described in the video, the vegetable garden undertaken with the PLP "freed up money [in her household] to buy some fruits or some meat." In another community, in the locality of Trancas, Tucumán, the main problem addressed by the project was childhood undernourishment. One of the women from civil society who participated in this project explained that the PLP had empowered her by teaching her how to provide nutritious meals to her children and educate other families on what she had learned: "I am proud of what I have done because my daughter was in third degree of [severe] malnutrition and now she is normal."

The following year, the second call for participatory local community projects proposals was out. The same guidelines were used to prioritize problems and identify addressable causes (see *Guía de Participación Local Participativa*). The funding for the 2007 PLPs came from an Interamerican Development Bank (IADB) loan of Argentine Pesos 1,000,000 (about USD 320,000). The ministry received 569 proposals, among which 201, as described next, were chosen following a careful double evaluation.

4.1 The Local Participatory Projects of 2007–2008

We chose to analyze the 2007–2008 PLPs for several reasons. First, the 2007 call for proposals had a very clear set of guidelines from the National Ministry of Health (elaborated upon from the previous year's guidelines) and for that reason the funded projects were well designed. The guidelines stated how the proposals had to be presented, and most importantly, how the community had to come up with the top-ranked problem related to public health (which was broadly defined to include issues of environment and sanitation) and how the community would seek to address such problem through the project. These guidelines also walked the CAPS personnel and communities through the ins and outs of participatory community planning. They were explicit about how to arrive to a local community diagnosis of the most pressing problems of the community, which could be addressed through community participation (as opposed to those that could not be addressed with these types of projects, such as unemployment or poverty). In terms of civil society activities, the PLPs promoted *consultation, planning, monitoring*, and *execution*. The recruitment was direct: any member of the community could participate. In fact, all health workers of the primary health care centers, professional and nonprofessional, were asked to work with community institutions and neighbors (*vecinos*). Finally, the guidelines also had clear criteria for what types of expenses were eligible and which expenses were not (for instance, only up to 20 percent of the budget could be allocated to human resources that were not part of the CAPS; CAPS personnel remuneration or CAPS infrastructure expenses were not eligible expenses, see *Guía de Participación Local Participativa,* 12–13).

The second reason that makes the 2007 PLPs particularly worthy of analysis is that because the call for proposals was extended to all the CAPS in Argentina, the 201 (one more than originally intended) funded projects were spread in localities throughout all the provinces of Argentina (see Map 1), instead of only in some of them, as it would be the case in future iterations of the PLP program.[36]

Finally, 2007 was the year for which we could find the most information available in the offices and archives of the National Ministry of Health. The available information consisted of dozens of two-ring five-inch filing folders containing photocopies of the projects proposals presented by the communities, the two independent project evaluations, the midterm evaluation of progress, the final evaluation, and in 121 cases the minutes of all the meetings that took place in the communities relating to the PLP projects, as well as some additional materials such as copies of receipts, and photos. All this information was available for 184 (91.5%) of all the funded projects.[37] One of the authors was allowed to consult and electronically compile that information.[38] This data was then combined with data from a Ministry of Health Census of CAPS of 2005.

The ministry received 569 proposals in 2007. Out of those proposals, 201 were selected after two independent evaluations. One evaluator was from the leading PLP team in the Ministry of Health. The other evaluator was either a member of the Red Cross or of Caritas (the two NGOs that had been working with the parent program REMEDIAR since 2002). The evaluation grid had very clear criteria about how to evaluate each proposal. These included: (1) methodology used to design the PLP (up to 25 points), (2) community participation (up to 35 points), (3) sanitary relevance (up to 20 points), (4) likelihood of continuity of the project (up to 10 points, in this item, if there existed support

---

[36] In 2009, the call for PLP proposals focused on the problem of dengue, which affected the provinces in northwestern Argentina. In 2010, the call for PLP proposals was restricted to those provinces that were signatories of another program called REDES.

[37] Unfortunately, hard copy records of seventeen funded projects were missing. This constitutes 8.5% of the total number of funded projects and we do not have information on why such records were missing. Moreover, the unfunded projects were archived outside of the ministry and we were not allowed access to those projects.

[38] In this task, the research assistants Luis Caiella and Luis Cecchi were absolutely instrumental. They compiled notes and recorded information on the 201 projects in the central offices' archives of the Ministry of Health during the nine-month period between August 2009 and March 2010. The resulting electronic database was shared with the Ministry of Health in late 2010.

Map 1 Distribution of 2007 Local Participatory Projects in Health, by
Locality, Argentina

from local authorities or other sources of financing, projects got more points),
and (5) creativity as a contribution to primary health care (APS) (up to 10
points). Each evaluator assigned a score between 0 and 100 to each proposal, by
filling out each section of the three-page evaluation questionnaire. The two
evaluations were averaged. The top-ranking 201 proposals were selected for
funding. We reviewed and compiled the scores of all the double evaluations of
the funded projects.[39] The two evaluations' averaged scores for the funded

---

[39] Although we did not have access to the evaluation of the unfunded projects, in the ministry
database of proposals, the unfunded projects had comments such as "there is no community
participation," "there are no community signatures," "it is not a participatory project," "40% of
the budget is for human resources," "over 10% of the expenses are not eligible," "incoherence
between causes and activities proposed," or "proposal does not follow the guidelines [or
methodology]."

projects varied from 60.5 to 98 points, with an average of 75.41 points. With regard to the evaluation of community participation (which could vary from 0 to 35 points), the average score was 25.15, with a minimum value of 13.8 and a maximum of 35 points. In comparing the community participation score given by the two evaluators (project participation score difference), the average difference was almost 3.1 points. These values are shown in Table 2, which also includes the summary statistics of all the other numerical variables analyzed in this section.

Everything in the archive materials of the ministry indicates that the evaluation process was based on merit and that there were no other considerations going into the decision of which projects to fund. Although in an interview, one of the members of the leading team recognized that the ministry tried to have at least one funded proposal in each province. This can be appreciated in Figure 2, which represents, in decreasing order, the number of funded proposals per province. The most populated province of Buenos Aires was granted thirty-six proposals. At the opposite end of the figure, the City of Buenos Aires, and the provinces of La Pampa, La Rioja, Santa Cruz, and Tierra del Fuego had one funded proposal each.

Each funded project received Argentine Pesos 5,000 (equivalent at the time to USD 1,600) to address the health-related problem identified as a first priority by the community. Half of the grant was paid to the community in July 2007 and the other half at the beginning of 2018, upon presentation of the first evaluation of progress of the project, which was conducted by the ministry PLP team, the Red Cross, Caritas, or the members of the community.

4.2 The Public Health Problems Tackled by the Communities

The first community participation task (required to draft the PLP proposal) was to brainstorm about the community health problems and their causes. Problems were defined as the distance between a real and an ideal situation, where the real situation was considered unsatisfactory. Moreover, as already mentioned, the problem had to be such that it could be addressed (*abordable*) with community participation (*Guía de planificación local participativa*, p. 6). Once the community chose the problem (following the guidelines' scoring system) and identified its addressable causes, the next step was to identify strategies and courses of action to address those causes. These courses of action had to be dealt with locally, with community participation, and within the boundaries of the available budget.[40]

---

[40] The *Guia de Participación Local Participativa* (p. 13) specified that expenses related to the design of the proposal, banking fees, CAPS' personnel remuneration, CAPS' ordinary expenses, and payment of debt were not eligible expenses.

Table 2 Summary Statistics

Variable	Mean	Minimum Value	Maximum Value	Standard Deviation	Number of Observations
Project Average Score	75.41	60.5	98	7.65	184
Project Participation Average Score	25.15	13.8	35	5.2	184
Project Participation Score Difference	3.07	0	15	3.42	183
Civil Society Participants in Project	8.53	0	39	5.63	184
Civil Society Women in Project	6.14	0	25	4.17	180
Civil Society Men in Project	2.38	0	14	2.51	180
Civil Society Participants in Final Report	6.06	0	29	4.73	115
Civil Society Women in Final Report	4.79	0	24	4.09	115
Civil Society Men in Final Report	1.27	0	8	1.55	115
Number of Meetings throughout Year	7.02	1	31	5.36	121
Average Number of Civil Society Participants in Meetings	4.53	0.11	31	4.49	118
Percentage of Budget Executed	79.92	18.5	100	21.51	123

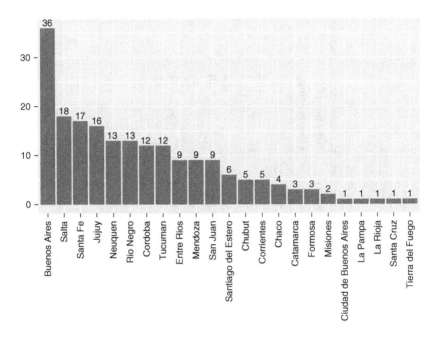

Figure 2 Number of Funded Proposals per Province

Among the funded proposals, the most common problem category was the environment (29 percent of the funded projects). These tended to be proposals having to do with the garbage treatment, sewage, and sanitation. Next were proposals addressing issues pertaining to adolescents (22 percent) and prenatal health (18 percent). Adolescence problems sometimes had to do with teenage pregnancies as well as unemployment. A series of other problem areas followed: chronic health problems (14 percent of the proposals), violence (7 percent, most common were projects referring to family violence), and senior citizens (4 percent) among others, as can be appreciated in Figure 3.

Most of these problems were reflective of poor communities. Examples of top-priority problems in poor or extremely poor communities included inadequate collection and disposal of trash, water contamination, lack of toilets in residences, young children malnourished and not achieving development markers for preschool admission, prevalence of teen pregnancies, drugs use (sometimes in the form of sniffing of glue compounds), alcohol abuse by teenagers, and lack of recreational opportunities for children and teenagers due to lack of common green areas or facilities such as gyms. In other (small number of) cases, projects sought to address problems related to the aged population, such as memory workshops or other recreational activities for retirees. Interestingly,

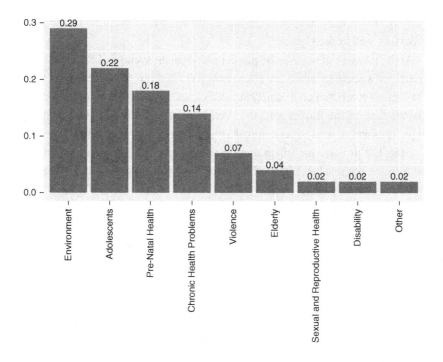

Figure 3 Categories of Problems Prioritized by Communities in PLPs (%)

these projects came from urban communities, such as Paraná in Entre Ríos, that we expect to be less afflicted by extreme poverty.

4.3 Who Participates and How Often?

The type of public health problems identified by communities and the supporting materials (photos, for instance) show that the PLPs resided largely in poor or extremely poor communities.[41] Moreover, the fact that the CAPS are mostly used by Argentines of low socioeconomic status (those who do not have health coverage by *obra social* or private health care) meant that the program was by design biased toward that sector of the population.

The original proposals as well as the final reports had to be signed by all the participants present at the meeting in which these documents were drafted. Through the counting of signatures and the coding of names of the signatories by gender, we can calculate the number of participants from civil society

---

[41] We merged our database with the Argentine 2001 national population census data. However, because the smallest unit we had recorded data for was the locality, we found the census information was not particularly helpful to describe the socioeconomic conditions of the immediate catchments of the CAPS.

present at the moment of signing the document and at the time of the final report, as well as their gender.[42]

At the moment of signing the project proposal, an average of 8.5 signatures from civil society members are found across the 184 projects. The project with the highest number of civil society signatures had 39 and the lowest had none.[43] By the time of the final report, the average number of civil society member signatures was 6, with a maximum of 29 signatures, and a minimum of none.[44] For the 112 projects for which there are signatures of civil society members both in the proposal and in the final report, we found that the correlation of number of participants is positive and statistically significant (r=0.29).

Regarding gender participation differences, as Figure 4 shows, among civic society participants, signatures of women participants were present at a larger ratio than men's signatures. At the time of the proposal design, the ratio was almost 3 women to 1 man (see left side of Figure 4). This is particularly significant because the proposal signatures reflect those who were present at the time of prioritizing problems within the community, the civil society activity we have called *planning*. At the time of the final report, the ratio was even larger in favor or women: almost 5 women to 1 man.

Why did woman participate disproportionately more than men in the PLPs? We believe the reason is that within the household division of labor, health care responsibilities predominantly follow under the purview of the women in the household.

In 121 of the projects carried out, there were meetings held throughout the year. The mode number of meetings held throughout the year is 3 and the

---

[42] In the Spanish language, female and male names are easily distinguishable. It is possible that this number underestimates the total number of participants who could have been present (some of them may have not signed). But there is no reason to believe that among those who did not sign, there would be a systematic gender bias – although it could be argued that in patriarchal societies such as many rural Argentine communities women would be less likely to sign than men. As we will see, women's signatures were disproportionately higher than men's.

[43] The project with thirty-nine signatures was from the CAPS 5926 from Villa San Isidro, Santa Maria, Córdoba. The title of the project was *El Rejunte, parte 2, con perfume de mujer*, which in English translates loosely as "The coming together, part 2, with [smell of] women's perfume." The part 2 in the title made reference to the fact that this CAPS had also won one of the 2006 PLPs, the title of which was "Recreating health." At the other end of the spectrum, there were six projects bearing no civil society signatures and only signatures from CAPS personnel (ranging from four to six CAPS personnel signatures).

[44] The final report with twenty-nine civil society member signatures was from CAPS 1520, from the locality and department of San Pedro, Jujuy. It targeted the neighborhood La Merced, where there were just over 5,400 inhabitants and twenty-five open-air trash-dumping sites. The project sought to build containers to dispose of household trash. Thirty-seven trash disposal containers were installed as a result of this community project; throughout the year, the members of the community met at least four times in relation to the execution of the project. At the other end of the spectrum, eight final reports did not include signatures from any member of civil society and were instead signed by CAPS personnel (in numbers ranging from three to nine signatures).

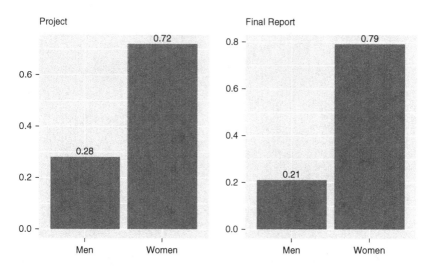

Figure 4 PLP's Participants by Gender

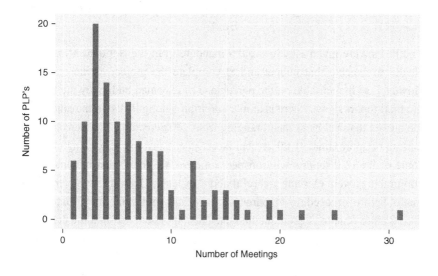

Figure 5 Number of Meetings Held Throughout the Year

median is 6. Few cases, which we call "super participants" and analyze later, had more than one meeting per month (see Figure 5). As for the number of civil society participants at these meetings, the average is between 4 and 5 people per meeting, with two outlier cases that had around or more than 20 participants per meeting (Figure 6).

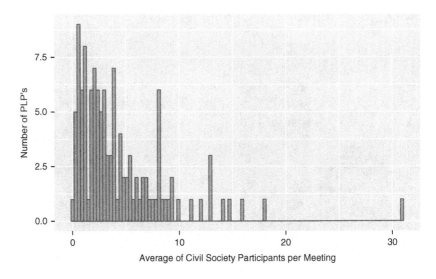

Figure 6 Average Number of Civil Society Participants in Meetings

4.4 How Does Programmatic Community Participation Work Best?

The PLPs were given a budget and a mandate from the National Ministry of Health to execute that budget and to complete the project within one year. However, as the variable on the percentage of executed budget by the time of the final report shows, there is ample variation among PLPs on the amount of the budget that had been spent, ranging from 100 percent to 18.5 percent, with a mean of approximately 80 percent (see Table 2, last row). Looking closer at some of the PLP reports with unspent moneys, we found that in some cases communities were extremely careful about expenses, looking for several estimates before proceeding to purchase materials, and sometimes that meant taking more time to execute the budget. Thus, it is not clear that the degree of execution of the budget is the best indicator to describe efficiency in the project, but it is the best approximate measure we have. Moreover, due to the relatively low number of cases and problems with missing data, we cannot estimate causal statistical models. However, to look more closely at the operation of the PLPs, we analyzed in further depth those projects that enjoyed a high level of participation of civil society.

4.5 What Do We Learn from the "Super Participants"?

To get a better grasp of the type and quality of participation in the PLPs, we now examine the group of programmatic participation community projects we call "super participants." These are the PLPs whose members met fifteen times or more throughout the year (representing about 5 percent of the total number of projects). From an in-depth study of these projects, and based solely on the information collected from the ministry (informed also by our in-depth interviews with national-level policy makers), we learn the following.

First, CAPS' employees act as bridging agents between communities and politicians on the local level. In some contexts (mostly rural), politicization is discouraged. For instance, the final report of a PLP in a rural community in the eastern part of the southern province of Neuquén (CAPS 3675, in Los Alamos, Plottier), a community consisting of 268 households that met 25 times throughout the year, stated that the principal problem they encounter was political. They explained that the project had to be placed on standby during the three months leading to the elections of October 2007:[45]

> The political parties approached us and tried to infiltrate us with political *punteros* [local vote getters or party brokers], who wanted to make themselves visible to the community. We decided not to be associated with [*no quedar pegados*] any party in particular and take some time off, instead ... From the get go we knew that if we stayed together they couldn't defeat us. There was also the problem that some people who came only wanted to participate in the project for politics. That was discouraging to us. We believe the decision to [temporarily] stop the project was the correct one. Now the project is in full-steam execution. (our translation from the original)

The title of this PLP was "The kids get lost, let's recover them." The main problem was the lack of activities for the kids and youth of the neighborhood, which was located at four kilometers from the center of the town of Plottier. The project sought to rehab a gymnasium that was abandoned and a soccer field. Among other tasks, the participants were able to negotiate with the electricity supply company to provide electricity to the gymnasium.[46] The PLP also offered classes of Tae kwon do, soccer, and a music concert throughout the year.

In other PLPs, the linkage with and help from the township was sought after and considered helpful. For example, just in the western outskirts of the City of

---

[45] These were the elections for president and national senators and deputies. The election for Neuquén's governor and state representatives had already taken place in early June of that year, before the start of the 2007 PLP projects in July.

[46] In fact, from the minutes of one of the meetings, we learned that this success had unintended consequences as some of the neighbors from nearby occupied lands requested that their houses be hooked up to the gymnasium electricity supply. The neighbors of Los Alamos, instead, more directly involved with the PLP opposed the request and asked to leave the discussion to another meeting (but the issue did not come up again in the minutes of future meetings).

Illustration 1 Trash container built by 2007 PLP "Reconstructing the Social Fabric: Everyone for a Healthy Environment," CAPS 11590, La Tablada, La Matanza, Province of Buenos Aires

Buenos Aires, in the Greater Buenos Aires neighborhood of Villa Insuperable, in the locality of La Matanza, Province of Buenos Aires, the members of the PLP, who met 22 times throughout the year, sought the support of the municipality to jointly decide the location of a large trash container (see Illustration 1) that was to be built with the PLP funding and the participating community.

The local secretary of social development participated in some of the meetings and the CAPS personnel acted as *bridgers* between the community and the local government.

Second, the programmatic participation of the community in the PLPs helped articulate and voice explicit societal demands to the local authorities. In both of the PLPs just cited (those corresponding to CAPS 3675 in Neuquén and CAPS 11590 in the Province of Buenos Aires), even if the approach or relationship with the local political leadership was different, both caps worked with the local government to channel the civil society demand for more sports programs in one case and for improving trash collection in the other.

Third, during the execution of the PLPs, a certain course of action or communal strategy could often lead to other activities that had not been originally included in the proposal but were nonetheless related to the problem tackled and part of its solution. An example of task transitions was from treatment of trash disposal to beautification of common green area and flattening the main dirt road of the neighborhood in the PLP of the CAPS 11590 in La Matanza, Province of Buenos Aires. Another example was the expansion of activities from the installation of toilets to the issue of cleaning the town water receptacles. This was the case of the PLP of CAPS 11361 in Campo Quijano, Rosario de Lerma, Salta. This community met twenty times during the year, built twenty-three indoor bathrooms, and later tackled other issues related to sanitation and the environment.

Fourth, in most projects, there were training or education components such as workshops aimed at the target populations but also their families, and frequently toward children. In fact, through the PLPs, the CAPS often advocate education and play for children. They opened their doors and went out to the community. Trust between community and the health care personnel increased. The communities also reported feeling more comfortable coming to their CAPS not only when they were sick but also seeking vaccination, other forms of preventive care, or other larger community-organizing goals.

4.6 The Aftermath of the Local Participatory Projects Program

In 2008, a change in the head of the ministry meant that the PLPs program was placed on standby. In 2009, the PLP leading team proposed to revive the program by targeting the problem of dengue. The country was facing the threat of a dengue epidemic that summer – outbreaks had already taken place in Brazil and in the north of Argentina. The leading authorities of the ministry agreed to the idea. Thus, the 2009 PLP program was geographically narrowed to the provinces most likely to be affected by dengue, in the center and north of Argentina.

With this change, the program not only lost geographic coverage but also its participatory *planning* component in that it narrowed the scope of problems that communities could seek to address to just one: fighting dengue. While the courses of action and strategies could vary, the prioritization of the problem was given by the state, not civil society. Thus, the program was shifting from a programmatic participatory program for policy making toward one that was narrower in the scope of civil society activities.

In 2010, in the context of a broader REMEDIAR + REDES program, the PLPs national team proposed to connect community networks directly with the provincial administrations. One of the shortcomings of the previous years, the national PLPs leading team thought, was the lack of cooperation between the provincial governments and the CAPS. The expanded REMEDIAR + REDES program provided the institutional "meso" or inter-mediate infrastructure: the regional or provincial networks that the PLPs could utilize. The funding international financial institutions (primarily the IADB and the World Bank) were skeptical of the utility of community participation in health and insisted on an evaluation of impact assessments.[47] Nonetheless, they funded the project in 2010 and the PLPs were launched in the subset of provinces that had signed on to the REDES program. Although by this point the program had lost its national coverage, it passed down the methodology for participatory planning and prioritization of community problems to the provinces.

At the national level, the PLPs were again under attack in 2012, and the program was discontinued. In 2015, under the auspices of a new minister of health, interested in having the ministry reach out to the local terri-tories, the PLPs program was revived and the National University of Sarmiento (a public university) in the greater Buenos Aires area became part of the national planning and evaluation team. However, according to different observers, the program was by then used mostly for electoral purposes, to continue building support for the government of Cristina Kirchner (2007–2011, 2011–2015) and for Daniel Scioli, who was running as her party's presidential candidate in the December elections of that year. In 2017, the new right wing and conservative government of Mauricio Macri decided to terminate the REMEDIAR program and with that, the PLPs program also ended.

---

[47] Interview with Andrea Casabal. August 1, 2017, Buenos Aires.

The fact that the program was designed and implemented from above meant that once the Ministry of Health and the national government authorities changed, the program could be terminated with a stroke of the pen. There has been some social resistance from CAPS personnel whose pay has been delayed or who are not contracted back by the State, but there has not been social mobilization to keep the program in place.

5 Conclusion

According to Charles Tilly (2005, 2007), one of the three prerequisites of democratization is the integration of societal trust networks into the State.[48] To democratize, Tilly argues, States must absorb private trust or, loosely defined, social capital into the public arena: there must be a broadening of popular participation (Tilly 2007, 138). It is in this process that civil society is integrated into the State and the State democratizes.

Since the Declaration of Alma-Ata, community involvement and initiatives to promote citizens' participation have flourished. As we saw in the first part of this Element, programmatic participation in public health was promoted in the context of democratization processes, whether in the form of transitions to democracy (Brazil and Chile), through the deepening of participatory democracy that was germane to the left turn in Latin America (Venezuela, Argentina, Bolivia, Ecuador), or through redistributive social revolutionary projects (Cuba). In these countries, we found that at least de jure, programmatic participation in health took the form of *programmatic participation for policy making*. This implied civil society activities beyond consultation and monitoring and also included planning and execution. We saw that the case of the local participatory projects in public health in Argentina in the mid-2000s was an example of this type of programmatic participation.

However, we also saw that programmatic participation in health could be the result of health system overhauls (Italy, Portugal, and Netherlands) or of sectoral decentralization processes (Colombia). Among these countries, programmatic participation in health had the characteristics of the type we labeled *programmatic participation for monitoring*. The population is consulted, but the decisions are not binding, and the primary role of civil society is to serve as watchdogs or evaluators of local-level provision of services. While there is no doubt that when properly taken into account, civil society input via monitoring can increase government accountability, we believe, as other scholars do (e.g., Pateman, 2012), that community participation for policy making is required if

---

[48] The other two prerequisites of democratization are (1) the insulation of public politics from categorical inequality and (2) the suppression of autonomous coercive power centers.

the integration of societal trust networks into the state is to perform a democratizing function.

Our analysis of local participatory projects (PLPs) in public health in Argentina has shown that sectoral elites were instrumental in the process of bringing about participatory institutions, just as Mayka (2019) has argued for the case of local health councils in Brazil, and as Harris (2017) has documented for the case of health reforms for universalization of access. Progressive policy makers acting on behalf of the interest of others brought about local participatory projects in Argentina, for instance, or local health councils in Brazil. However, we believe it was precisely the lack of an organized social movement behind those leaders that meant that the PLP program was short lived and highly dependent on the political will of national leaders. Instead, as shown elsewhere (Falleti and Riofrancos, 2018), when participatory institutions come about by societal demand and the sectors mobilized for their adoption are politically incorporated, participatory institutions are more likely to be implemented, enforced, and strengthened over time.

Regarding the PLP program, we have also shown that this program targeted poor populations. Unlike other forms of political participation, programmatic participation in public health in the developing world may indeed be a means of incorporating the neediest sectors of the population. We also found that in mostly poor and rural or semi-urban settings, women participated more than men both at the stage of prioritizing problems in health and at the end of the process. In at least one of the PLPs, women reported feeling empowered as a result of the knowledge acquired through the PLP and the new opportunities for leadership and volunteering in their communities. However, such civil society engagement or incorporation is not unmediated. As we found out, health personnel were key brokers (or "bridgers") between communities and the larger bureaucracy of the State in health as well as with the local political authorities. They could keep clientelistic impulses from local politicians at bay and prevent, in some cases, the co-optation of the projects for partisan or particularistic gains.

The analysis of the PLP program also showed the importance of a clear, well-designed set of guidelines to prioritize problems, and to identify addressable causes and strategies of programmatic community participatory action. Finally, we found no evidence in the PLPs that a synergetic relationship between representatives and citizens was required for meaningful participation. The linkage that mattered most was that between community and health care personnel. The relationship with the municipalities or local authorities was synergetic and productive at times, or conflict ridden and unproductive in other cases. In either case, the degree of community involvement in the project and its successful implementation were not correlated with participation by the municipal authorities.

Is programmatic participation in health a panacea? Certainly not. As we saw in the comparative cross-country analysis, participation does not always mean inclusion. Several scholars highlighted the problem of biased representation toward health providers or patients' organizations with more knowledge and resources, as in the cases of Italy, Portugal, and the Netherlands, for instance. In the case of PLPs in Argentina, we also found that the relationship between programmatic community participation at the local level and political leadership is a complex one. Threatened by rising new leaderships, local political leaders may compete with programmatic participation or attempt to co-opt it. More research is necessary to better understand the local context conditions that lead to either collaborative or competitive incentives between organized communities and local politicians. Despite these areas of uncertainty, the PLPs in Argentina did bring, through programmatic community participation, coordinated by the health personnel, solutions to communities that badly needed them and provided them with organizational tools that survived the scope of the projects. These results possibly bode well for those institutional innovations for community participation in public health systems that were brought about by political reform processes, at least where they have not reached exhaustion (Venezuela) or elimination (Argentina). It also shows the potential that institutions of programmatic participation for civic monitoring may have if they are expanded to include more civil society activities and to grant civil society more of a role in policy making.

References

Abers, Rebecca Neaera 2000. *Inventing Local Democracy: Grassroots Politics in Brazil*, Boulder, CO: Lynne Rienner Publishers, Inc.

Abers, Rebecca Neaera & Keck, Margaret E. 2013. *Practical Authority. Agency and Institutional Change in Brazilian Water Politics*, New York and Oxford: Oxford University Press.

Acuña, Carlos & Chudnovsky, Mariana 2002. *El sistema de salud en Argentina. Documento N° 60.* Buenos Aires: Universidad de San Andrés.

Almond, Gabriel A. 1980. The Intellectual History of the Civic Culture Concept. *In:* Almond, Gabriel A. & Verba, Sidney (eds.) *The Civic Culture Revisited.* Boston and Toronto: Little, Brown, 1–36.

Almond, Gabriel & Verba, Sidney 1963. *The Civic Culture: Political Attitudes and Democracy in Five Nations*, Princeton, NJ: Princeton University Press.

Altschuler, Daniel & Corrales, Javier 2012. The Spillover Effects of Participatory Governance: Evidence from Community-Managed Schools in Honduras and Guatemala. *Comparative Political Studies*, 45 (5), 636–666.

Anigstein, Carlos 2007. Modalidades de participación ciudadana. *Revista ISalud*, 2, 31–36.

Armada, F., Muntaner, C., Chung, H., Williams-Brennan, L., & Benach, J. 2009. Barrio Adentro and the Reduction of Health Inequalities in Venezuela: An Appraisal of the First Years. *International Journal of Health Services*, 39, 161–187.

Arretche, Marta T. S. 1999. Políticas Sociais no Brasil: descentralização em um Estado federativo. *Revista Brasileira de Ciências Sociais*, 14, 111–141.

Artaza-Barrios, Osvaldo, Toro-Devia, O., Fuentes-García, A., Alarcón-Hein, A. & Arteaga-Herrera, O. 2013. Gobierno de redes asistenciales: evaluación de los Consejos Integradores de la Red Asistencial (CIRA) en el contexto de la reforma del sector salud en Chile. *Salud Pública de México*, 55, 650–658.

Avritzer, Leonardo 2009. *Participatory Institutions in Democratic Brazil*, Washington DC: Woodrow Wilson Center Press.

Azevedo, Carlos Antonio 1998. La provisión de servicios de salud en Chile: aspectos históricos, dilemas y perspectivas. *Revista de Saúde Pública*, 32, 192–199.

Baiocchi, Gianpaolo & Ganuza, Ernesto 2015. Becoming a Best Practice: Neoliberalism and the Curious Case of Participatory Budgeting. *In:* Lee, Caroline W., Mcquarrie, Michael, & Walker, Edward T. (eds.) *Democratizing Inequalities: Dilemmas of the New Public Participation.* New York: New York University Press, 192–198.

Baiocchi, Gianpaolo & Ganuza, Ernesto 2017. *Popular Democracy. The Paradox of Participation*, Stanford, CA: Stanford University Press.

Baiocchi, Gianpaolo, Heller, Patrick, & Silva, Marcelo 2011. *Bootstrapping Democracy: Transforming Local Governance and Civil Society in Brazil*, Stanford, CA: Stanford University Press.

Baldini, Gianfranco & Baldi, Brunetta 2014. Decentralization in Italy and the Troubles of Federalization. *Regional & Federal Studies*, 24, 87–108.

Becerril-Montekio, Víctor, Reyes, Juan De Dios, & Manuel, Annick 2011. Sistema de salud de Chile. *Salud Pública de México*, 53, 132–142.

Berlotto, Analía, Fuks, Ana, & Rovere, Mario 2012. Primary Health care in Argentina: disordered proliferation and conflicting models. *Saúde em Debate*, 36, 362–374.

Björkman, Martina & Svensson, Jakob 2009. Power to the People: Evidence from a Randomized Field Experiment on Community-Based Monitoring in Uganda. *The Quarterly Journal of Economics*, 124, 735–769.

Blank, R., Burau, V., & Kuhlmann, E. 2017. *Comparative Health Policy*, London: Palgrave.

Bonvecchio, Anabelle, Becerril-Montekio, Victor, Carriedo-Lutzenkirchen, Ángela, & Landaeta-Jiménez, Maritza 2011. Sistema de salud de Venezuela. *Salud Pública de México*, 53, 275–286.

Booth, John A. 1979. Political Participation in Latin America: Levels, Structure, Context, Concentration and Rationality. *Latin American Research Review*, 14, 29–60.

Booth, John A. & Seligson, Mitchell A. 1978. Images of Political Participation in Latin America. *In:* Booth, John A. & Seligson, Mitchell A. (eds.) *Political Participation in Latin America*. Vol. I, Citizen and State. New York: Holmes & Meier Publishers, Inc, 3–33.

Brinks, Daniel, Levitsky, Steven, & Murillo, Maria Victoria 2018. Understanding Weak Institutions: Lessons from Latin America., Book manuscript, Columbia University.

Brown, Lawrence 1984. Health Reform, Italian-style. *Health Affairs*, 3, 75–101.

Cameron, Maxwell A., Hershberg, Eric, & Sharpe, Kenneth E. 2012. *New Institutions for Participatory Democracy in Latin America. Voice and Consequence*, New York: Palgrave Macmillan.

Cammett, Melani 2014. *Compassionate Communalism: Welfare and Sectarianism in Lebanon*, Ithaca, NY: Cornell University Press.

Cammett, Melani & Maclean, Lauren (eds.) 2014. *The Politics of Non-state Social Welfare*, Ithaca, NY: Cornell University Press.

Carpenter, Daniel 2012. Is Health Politics Different? *Annual Review of Political Science*, 15, 287–311.

Carvajal, Jairo. 2016. *Gestión de la participación social y comités locales de salud. Estudio de caso del Comité Local de Salud del Circuito Ciudad Nueva*. M.A. in Health Management, Universidad Central del Ecuador.

Cetrángolo, Oscar & Jiménez, Juan Pablo 2003. *Política fiscal en Argentina durante el régimen de convertibilidad*. Santiago de Chile: Instituto Latinoamericano y del Caribe de Planificación Económica y Social, ILPES, and Buenos Aires office of the Comisión Económica para América Latina y el Caribe, CEPAL.

Coelho Schattan, Vera 2005. Los consejos de salud en Brasil: ¿cuánto hemos avanzado en la concertación de intereses? *Revista del CLAD Reforma y Democracia*, 32, 1–11.

Cohu, Sylvie, Lequet-Slama, Diane, & Volovitch, Pierre 2006. The Netherlands: Reform of the Health System Based on Competition and Privatisation. *Revue française des affaires sociales*, 6, 207–226.

Collier, Ruth Berins & Handlin, Samuel (eds.) 2009. *Reorganizing Popular Politics. Participation and the New Interest Regime in Latin America*, University Park: The Pennsylvania State University.

Conill, E., Minayo, M., Akerman, M., Drumond Júnior, M., & Carvalho, Y. 2006. Sistemas comparados de saúde. *Saúde em Debate*, 170, 563–613.

Cooke, Bill & Kothari, Uma 2001. *Participation: The New Tyranny?* London: Zed Books.

Cornwall, Andrea 2008. Deliberating Democracy: Scenes from a Brazilian Municipal Health Council. *Politics & Society*, 36, 508–531.

Crisóstomo, Sofia, Matos, Ana, Borges, Marta, & Santos, Margarida 2017. Mais participação, melhor saúde: um caso de ativismo virtual na saúde. *Forum Sociológico*, 2, 7–16.

Davies, Emmerich & Falleti, Tulia G. 2017. Poor People's Participation: Neoliberal Institutions or Left Turn? *Comparative Political Studies*, 50, 1699–1731.

De Vos, Pol, Malaise, G., De Ceukelaire, W., Perez, D., Lefèvre, P., & Van Der Stuyft, P. 2009. Participation and Empowerment in Primary Health Care: From Alma-Ata to the Era of Globalization. *Social Medicine*, 4, 121–127.

Delamaza, Gonzalo & Ochsenius, Carlos 2010. Redes de participación institucional y gobernanza democrática local. El caso de los Presupuestos

Participativos en Chile. *Revista del CLAD Reforma y Democracia*, 46, 213–246.

Delgado-Gallego, María & Vázquez-Navarrete, Luisa 2006. Barreras y oportunidades para la participación social en salud en Colombia: percepciones de los actores principales. *Revista de Salud Pública*, 8, 128–140.

Den Exter, André, Hermans, H., Dosljak, M., Busse, R., Ginneken, E., & Schreyoegg, J. 2004. *Health Care Systems in Transition: Netherlands*. Copenhagen: WHO Regional Office for Europe on behalf of the European Observatory on Health Systems and Policies.

Domínguez-Alonso, Emma & Zacea, Eduardo 2011. Sistema de salud de Cuba. *Salud Pública de México*, 53, 168–176.

Dunning, Thad 2009. Direct Action and Associational Participation: Problem-Solving Repertoires of Individuals. *In:* Collier, Ruth Berins & Handlin, Samuel (eds.) *Reorganizing Popular Politics. Participation and the New Interest Regime in Latin America*. University Park: The Pennsylvania State University Press, 95–131.

Eaton, Kent 2002. *Politicians and Economic Reform in New Democracies: Argentina and the Philippines in the 1990s*, University Park: The Pennsylvania State University Press.

Eaton, Kent 2004. *Politics Beyond the Capital: The Design of Subnational Institutions in South America*, Stanford, CA: Stanford University Press.

Eaton, Kent 2014. Recentralization and the Left Turn in Latin America: Diverging Outcomes in Bolivia, Ecuador, and Venezuela. *Comparative Political Studies*, 47, 1130–1157.

Ellner, Steve 2008. *Rethinking Venezuelan Politics: Class, Conflict, and the Chávez Phenomenon*, Boulder, CO: Lynne Rienner.

Ewig, Christina 2010. *Second-Wave Neoliberalism: Gender, Race, and Health Sector Reform in Peru*, University Park: The Pennsylvania State University Press.

Faguet, Jean-Paul 2012. *Decentralization and Popular Democracy: Governance from Below in Bolivia*, Ann Arbor: University of Michigan Press.

Faguet, Jean-Paul 2014. Decentralization and Governance. *World Development*, 53, 2–13.

Falleti, Tulia G. 2005. A Sequential Theory of Decentralization: Latin American Cases in Comparative Perspective. *American Political Science Review*, 99, 327–346.

Falleti, Tulia G. 2010a. *Decentralization and Subnational Politics in Latin America*, New York: Cambridge University Press.

Falleti, Tulia G. 2010b. Infiltrating the State: The Evolution of Health Care Reforms in Brazil, 1964–1988 *In:* Mahoney, James & Thelen, Kathleen (eds.) *Explaining Institutional Change: Ambiguity, Agency, and Power.* New York: Cambridge University Press, 38–62.

Falleti, Tulia G. & Riofrancos, Thea N. 2018. Endogenous Participation: Strengthening Prior Consultation In Extractive Economies. *World Politics*, 70, 86–121.

Faust, Jörg & Harbers, Imke 2011. On the Local Politics of Administrative Decentralization: Applying for Policy Responsibilities in Ecuador. *Publius: The Journal of Federalism*, 42, 52–77.

Feinsilver, Julie 1993. *Healing the Masses: Cuban Health Politics at Home and Abroad*, Berkeley, California, University of California Press.

Ferré, F., De Belvis, A., Valerio, L., Longhi, S., Lazzari, A., Fattore, G., Ricciardi, W. & Maresso, A. 2014. Italy: Health System Review. *Health Systems in Transition*, 16, 1–168.

Fornos, Carolina A., Power, Timothy J., & Garand, James C. 2004. Explaining Voter Turnout in Latin America, 1980 to 2000. *Comparative Political Studies*, 37, 909–940.

Frenz, Patricia, Alfaro, Tania, & Mazzei, Marinella. 2017. *Case Study: Citizen Participation and Co-Management for Health in Chile.* In: *The Shaping Health Programme on Learning from International Experience on Approaches to Community Power, Participation and Decision-Making in Health*, Santiago de Chile: Universidad de Chile, TARSC.

Fundación Centro Gumilla 2009. Estudio cuantitativo de opinión sobre los Consejos Comunales. Caracas, Venezuela: Fundación Centro Gumilla.

Fung, Archon & Wright, Erik Olin (eds.) 2003. *Deepening Democracy: Institutional Innovations in Empowered Participatory Governance*, New York: Verso Books.

Galindo, Mario 2016. *La Participación Ciudadana y el Control Social*, La Paz: CEBEM.

Galindo, Mario & Medina, Fernando 1995. *Descentralización fiscal en Bolivia.* Proyecto Regional de Descentralización Fiscal de las Naciones Unidas Serie Politica Fiscal 72.

Goldfrank, Benjamin 2007a. Lessons from Latin America's Experience with Participatory Budgeting. *In:* Shah, Anwar (ed.) *Participatory Budgeting.* Washington, DC: The World Bank, 91–126.

Goldfrank, Benjamin 2007b. The Politics of Deepening Local Democracy. Decentralization, Party Institutionalization, and Participation. *Comparative Politics*, 39, 147–168.

Goldfrank, Benjamin 2011. *Deepening Local Democracy in Latin America. Participation, Decentralization, and the Left*, University Park: The Pennsylvania State University Press.

Gonzalez, Yanilda 2016. Varieties of Participatory Security: Assessing Community Participation in Policing in Latin America. *Public Administration and Development*, 26, 132–143.

Goss, Claudia, & Renzi, Cristina. 2007. Patient and citizen participation in health care decisions in Italy. *Z.ärztl. Fortbild. Qual.Gesundh.wes. (ZaeFQ)*, 101, 236–240.

Grindle, Merilee 2000. *Audacious Reforms: Institutional Invention and Democracy in Latin America*, Baltimore and London: John Hopkins University Press.

Guerrero, Ramiro, Gallego, Ana Isabel, Becerril-Montekio, Victor, & Vásquez, Johanna 2011. Sistema de salud de Colombia. *Salud Pública de México*, 53, 144–155.

Haasnoot, Robbert. 2012. Decentralization of Dutch Nature Policy: Opportunities and Threats for Nature. Master's Thesis, Utrecht University.

Hadjez-Berrios, Esteban 2014. A Socio-psychological Perspective on Community Participation in Health during the Unidad Popular Government: Santiago de Chile, from 1970 to 1973. *Journal of Health Psychology*, 19, 90–96.

Han, Hahrie 2009. *Moved to Action. Motivation, Participation, and Inequality in American Politics*, Stanford, CA: Stanford University Press.

Hanson, Rebecca 2018. Deepening Distrust: Why Participatory Experiments Are Not Always Good for Democracy. *The Sociological Quarterly*, 59, 145–167.

Harris, Joseph 2017. *Achieving Access. Professional Movements and the Politics of Health Universalism*, Ithaca: Cornell University Press.

Heller, Patrick 2001. Moving the State: The Politics of Democratic Decentralization in Kerala, South Africa, and Porto Alegre. *Politics & Society*, 29, 131–163.

Hernández, Mario 2002. Reforma sanitaria, equidad y derecho a la salud en Colombia. *Cadernos de Saúde Pública*, 18, 991–1001.

Hevia De La Jara, Felipe J., & Isunza Vera, Ernesto 2012. Constrained Participation: The Impact of Consultative Councils on National-Level Policy in Mexico. *In:* Cameron, Maxwell A., Hershberg, Eric, & Sharpe, Kenneth E. (eds.) *New Institutions for Participatory Democracy in Latin America*. New York: Palgrave Macmillan, 75–97.

Hiskey, Jonathan & Seligson, Mitchell 2003. Pitfalls of power to the people: Decentralization, local government performance, and system support in Bolivia. *Studies in Comparative International Development*, 37, 64–88.

Humphreys, Macartan, Sanchez De La Sierra, Raul, & Van Der Windt, Peter 2012. Social and Economic Impacts of Tuungane. Final Report on the Effects of a Community Driven Reconstruction Program in Eastern Democratic Republic of Congo. Columbia University.

Israr, Syed & Islam, Anwar 2006. Good Governance and Sustainability: A Case Study from Pakistan. *The International Journal of Health Planning and Management*, 21, 313–325.

Jara, Claudio & Torres Andrade, Cristina 2015. Participación en salud y desarrollo territorial: Experiencia sanitaria en una comuna del Sur de Chile. *Ciencia y enfermería*, 21, 115–125.

Keck, William & Reed, Gail 2012. The Curious Case of Cuba. *American Journal of Public Health*, 102, 13–22.

Kelly, Ann, Macgregor, Hayley, & Montgomery, Catherine 2017. The Publics Of Public Health In Africa. *Critical Public Health*, 27, 1–5.

Kohl, Benjamin 2003. Democratizing Decentralization in Bolivia – The Law of Popular Participation. *Journal of Planning Education and Research*, 23, 153–164.

Krishna, Anirudh 2006. Poverty and Democratic Participation Reconsidered: Evidence from the Local Level in India. *Comparative Politics* 38, 439–458.

Labra, Maria Eliana 2002. Capital social y consejos de salud en Brasil:¿ un círculo virtuoso? *Cadernos de saúde pública*, 18, 47–55.

Labra, Maria Eliana 2005. Conselhos de Saúde: dilemas, avanços e desafios. *In:* Lima, Nísia Trinidade, Gerschman, Silvia, Coelho Edler, Flavio, & Suárez, Julio Manuel (eds.) *Saúde e Democracia. História e perspectivas do SUS*. Rio de Janeiro: Editora Fiocruz, 353–383.

Lamping, Antonie, Raab, Jörg, & Kenis, Patrick 2012. Participation and Coordination in Dutch Health Care Policy-Making. A Network Analysis of the System of Intermediate Organizations in Dutch Health Care. *Health Promotion International*, 28, 211–222.

Ledo, Carmen & Soria, René 2011. Sistema de salud de Bolivia. *Salud Pública de México*, 53, 109–119.

Lima, Nísia Trindade, Lima, N., Gerschman, S., Edler, F., & Suárez, J. 2005. *Saúde e democracia: história e perspectivas do SUS*, Rio de Janeiro, Brazil, Editora FIOCRUZ.

Lucio, Ruth, Villacrés, Nilhda, & Henríquez, Rodrigo 2011. Sistema de salud de Ecuador. *Salud Pública de México*, 53, 177–187.

Lupien, Pascal 2018. *Citizens' Power in Latin America: Theory and Practice*, Albany: State University of New York Press.

Matos, Ana Raquel & Serapioni, Mauro 2017. The Challenge of Citizens' Participation in Health Systems in Southern Europe: A Literature Review. *Cadernos de saude publica*, 33, 1–10.

Mayka, Lindsay 2019. *Building Participatory Institutions in: Latin America. Reform Coalitions and Institutional Change*, New York: Cambridge University Press.

Mcadam, Doug, Tarrow, Sidney, & Tilly, Charles 2001. *Dynamics of Contention*, New York: Cambridge University Press.

McNulty, Stephanie L. 2011. *Voice and Vote: Decentralization and Participation in Post-Fujimori Peru*, Stanford, CA: Stanford University Press.

Meier, Benjamin, Pardue, Caitlin, & London, Leslie 2012. Implementing Community Participation through Legislative Reform: A Study of the Policy Framework for Community Participation in the Western Cape Province of South Africa. *BMC International Health and Human Rights*, 12, 15.

Ministerio de Salud de Bolivia 2015. *Guía de procedimientos de la gestión participativa municipal en salud*, La Paz: Servicios Integrales Victoria.

Ministry of Health of Ecuador 2007. Guía metodológica para la elaboración de los planes cantonales y provinciales de salud. Quito.

Ministry of Health Welfare and Sport 2011. Health Insurance in the Netherlands. The Netherlands: The Hague.

Montekio, Víctor, Medina, Guadalupe, & Aquino, Rosana 2011. Sistema de salud de Brasil. *Salud Pública de México*, 53, 120–131.

Montero, Alfred P. & Samuels, David J. 2004. The Political Determinants of Decentralization in Latin America. Causes and Consequences. *In:* Montero, Alfred P. & Samuels, David J. (eds.) *Decentralization and Democracy in Latin America*. Notre Dame, IN: University of Notre Dame Press, 3–32.

Moran, M. 1999. *Governing the Health Care State: A Comparative Study of the United Kingdom, the United States and Germany*, Manchester: Manchester University Press.

Moran, M. 2000. Understanding the Welfare State: The Case of Health Care. *The British Journal of Politics and International Relations*, 2, 135–160.

Moreira, Marcelo & Escorel, Sarah 2009. Municipal Health Councils of Brazil: A Debate on the Democratization of Health in the Twenty Years of the UHS. *Ciência & Saúde Coletiva*, 14, 795–806.

Murthy, Ranjani & Klugman, Barbara 2004. Service Accountability and Community Participation in the Context of Health Sector Reforms in Asia: Implications for Sexual and Reproductive Health Services. *Health Policy and Planning*, 19, i78–i86.

Navarro, Vicente 1974. What Does Chile Mean: An Analysis of Events in the Health Sector Before, During, and After Allende's Administration. *The Milbank Memorial Fund Quarterly. Health and Society*, 52, 93–130.

Nguyen, Vinh-Kim 2010. *The Republic of Therapy: Triage and Sovereignty in West Africa's Time of AIDS*, Durham, NC: Duke University Press.

Noboa, Hugo, Salas, Bernarda, Neira, Tatiana, & Betancourt, Zaida 2011. Investigaćion operativa: El rol de los-as usuarios-as organizados-as en la mejora de la atenćion de salud en el Ecuador. Quito: Participaćion y calidad de atenćion en salud, Ecuador.

Nunes, J., Matias, M., & Filipe, Â. 2007. Patient Organizations as Emerging Actors in the Health Arena: The Case of Portugal. *RECIIS: Electronic Journal of Communication, Information & Innovation in Health*, 1, 105–108.

Nunes Silva, Carlos 2017. Political and Administrative Decentralization in Portugal: Four Decades of Democratic Local Government. *In:* Nunes Silva, Carlos & Buček, J. (eds.) *Local Government and Urban Governance in Europe*. Cham, Switzerland: Springer, 9–32.

Olson, Mancur 1968. *The Logic of Collective Action: Public Goods and the Theory of Groups*, Cambridge, MA: Harvard University Press.

Pan-American Health Organization 2001. Perfil del sistema de servicios de salud de Cuba. Programa de Organización y Gestión de Sistemas y Servicios de Salud División de Desarrollo de Sistemas y Servicios de Salud, La Habana, Cuba.

Pateman, Carole 2012. Participatory Democracy Revisited, APSA 2011 Presidential Address. *Perspectives on Politics*, 10, 7–19.

Pérez-Linán, Aníbal 2001. Neoinstitutional Accounts of Voter Turnout: Moving Beyond Industrial Democracies. *Electoral Studies*, 20, 281–297.

Pogrebinschi, Thamy 2012. Participation as Representation: Democratic Policymaking in Brazil. *In:* Cameron, Maxwell A., Hershberg, Eric, & Sharpe, Kenneth E. (eds.) *New Institutions for Participatory Democracy in Latin America*. New York: Palgrave Macmillan, 53–74.

Pogrebinschi, Thamy 2013. The Squared Circle of Participatory Democracy: Scaling Up Deliberation to the National Level. *Critical Policy Studies*, 7, 219–241.

Pogrebinschi, Thamy & Samuels, David 2014. The Impact of Participatory Democracy: Evidence from Brazil's National Public Policy Conferences. *Comparative Politics*, 46, 313–332.

Putnam, Robert D. 1993. *Making Democracy Work: Traditions in Modern Italy*, Princeton, NJ: Princeton University Press.

Putnam, Robert D. 2000. *Bowling Alone. The Collapse and Revival of American Community*, New York: Simon & Schuster.

Redes, 2012. *Remediar+Redes. 10 años comprometidos con la salud pública.* Buenos Aires: Ministerio de Salud de la Nación.

Remmer, Karen L. 2009. Political Scale and Electoral Turnout: Evidence from the Less Industrialized World. *Comparative Political Studies*, 43, 275–303.

Restrepo, D., Palacio, G., Novoa, E., & Gonzalez, J. 1996. *Globalización y Estado Nación*, Bogotá: Escuela Superior de Administración Pública.

Rifkin, Susan 1986. Lessons from Community Participation in Health Programmes. *Health Policy and Planning*, 1, 240–249.

Rifkin, Susan 2009. Lessons from Community Participation in Health Programmes: A Review of the Post Alma-Ata Experience. *International Health*, 1, 31–36.

Rosen, George 1957. *A History of Public Health*, New York: MD Publications, Inc.

Saez González, Raquel 2013. Modalidades latinoamericanas de participación social en salud. *Cuestiones Políticas*, 29, 41–64.

Saez González, Raquel 2015. Participación social en salud. Un análisis político y normativo. *Cuestiones Políticas*, 31, 131–158.

Sanabria Ramos, Gisela & Benavides López, Maryeline 2003. Evaluación del movimiento de municipios por la salud: Playa, 2001. *Revista Cubana de Salud Pública*, 29, 139–146.

Sanabria Ramos, Gisela 2004. Participación social en el campo de la salud. Revista Cubana de Salud Pública [online], No. 30 (July-September), accessible at www.redalyc.org/articulo.oa?id=21430305 ISSN 0864-3466, last consulted 09/24/18.

Schäfer, Willemijn, Kronema, M., Boerma, W., Van Den Berg, M., Westert, G., Devillé, W., & Van Ginneken, E. 2010. The Netherlands: Health System Review. *Health Systems in Transition*, 12, 1–228.

Schmitt, Carina 2010. Sources of Civic Engagement in Latin America: Empirical Evidence from Rural Ecuadorian Communities. *Journal of Development Studies*, 46, 1442–1458.

Seligson, Mitchell A. & Booth, John A. 1976. Political Participation in Latin America: An Agenda for Research. *Latin American Research Review*, 11, 95–119.

Selnes, T. & Kuindersma, W. 2006. Ruimte voor elkaar. Een essay over decentralisatie in het natuurbeleid. Rapport, 7.

Sen, Amartya 1999. *Commodities and Capabilities*, Oxford: Oxford University Press.

Serapioni, Mauro & Duxbury, Nancy 2014. Citizens' Participation in the Italian Health-Care System: The Experience of the Mixed Advisory Committees. *Health Expectations*, 17, 488–499.

Serapioni, Mauro & Matos, Ana Raquel 2014. Citizen Participation and Discontent in Three Southern European Health Systems. *Social Science & Medicine*, 123, 226–233.

Serrano, Claudia & Acosta, Patricia 2011. "El proceso de descentralización en el Ecuador." Proyecto gobernanza subnacional para el desarrollo territorial en Los Andes. Quito, Ecuador.

Silva, Herland Tejerina, Soors, Werner, De Paepe, Pierre, Aguilar Santacruz, Edison, Closon, Marie-Christine, & Unger, Jean-Pierre 2009. Reformas de gobiernos socialistas a las políticas de salud en Bolivia y Ecuador: el potencial subestimado de la Atención Primaria Integral de Salud para impactar los determinantes sociales en salud. *Medicina social*, 4, 273–282.

Simões, J., Augusto, G., Fronteira, I., & Hernández-Quevedo, C. 2017. Portugal: Health System Review. *Health Systems in Transition*, 19, 1–184.

Sintomer, Yves, Herzberg, Carsten, & Rocke, Anja 2010. Learning from the South: Participatory Budgeting Worldwide – an Invitation to Global Cooperation. Dialog Global, 25.

Skocpol, Theda 1979. *States and Social Revolutions: A Comparative Analysis of France, Russia, and China*, New York: Cambridge University Press.

Smith, Graham 2009. *Democratic Innovations. Designing Institutions for Citizen Participation*, New York: Cambridge University Press.

Souza, Celina 2001. Participatory Budgeting In Brazilian Cities: Limits and Possibilities in Building Democratic Institutions. *Environment and Urbanization*, 13, 159–184.

Souza, Celina 2004. Governos locais e gestão de políticas sociais universais. *São Paulo em Perspectiva*, 18, 27–41.

Spiegel, J., Alegret, M., Clair, V., Pagliccia, N., Martinez, B., Bonet, M., & Yassi, A. 2012. Intersectoral Action for Health at a Municipal Level in Cuba. *International Journal of Public Health* 57, 15–23.

Sugiyama, Natasha Borges 2008. Theories of Policy Diffusion: Social Sector Reform in Brazil. *Comparative Political Studies*, 41, 193–216.

Tarrow, Sidney 2008 [1998]. *Power in Movement. Social Movements and Contentious Politics*, New York: Cambridge University Press.

Teruggi, Marco Augusto. 2012. *Los consejos comunales en Venezuela (2006–2010): Análisis de una experiencia de organización y participación impulsada por el Estado, desde la perspectiva del poder popular.* B.A. in Sociology, Universidad Nacional de La Plata.

Tilly, Charles 2005. *Trust and Rule*, New York: Cambridge University Press.

Tilly, Charles 2007. *Democratization*, New York: Cambridge University Press.

Tobar, Federico 2006. Descentralización y reformas de salud en América Latina. *In:* Yadón, Zaida (ed.) *Descentralización y gestión del control de las enfermedades transmisibles en América Latina.* Buenos Aires: Organización Panamericana de la Salud, 65–114.

Tobar, Federico 2012. Breve historia del sistema argentino de salud. *In:* Garay, Oscar (ed.) *Responsabilidad Profesional de los Médicos. Ética, Bioética y Jurídica. Civil y Penal.* Buenos Aires: La Ley, 1287–1337.

Toonen, Theo 1987. The Netherlands: A Decentralised Unitary State in a Welfare Society. *West European Politics*, 10, 108–129.

Torri, Maria Costanza 2012. Multicultural Social Policy and Community Participation in Health: New Opportunities and Challenges for Indigenous People. *The International Journal of Health Planning and Management*, 27, 18–40.

Tranjan, Ricardo J. 2016. *Participatory Democracy in Brazil. Socioeconomic and Political Origins*, Notre Dame, IN: University of Notre Dame Press.

Tsai, Lily L. 2007. Solidary Groups, Informal Accountability, and Local Public Goods Provision in Rural China. *American Political Science Review*, 101, 355–372.

Tuohy, C. 2003. Agency, Contract, and Governance: Shifting Shapes of Accountability in the Health Care Arena. *Journal of Health Politics, Policy and Law*, 28, 195–215.

Uzcategui, José 2012. *La participación ciudadana en salud en Venezuela y el nuevo marco constitucional: ¿de la representatividad a la participación protagónica?*, Carabobo: Universidad de Carabobo.

Van De Bovenkamp, Hester, Trappenburg, M., & Grit, K. 2010. Patient Participation in Collective Healthcare Decision Making: The Dutch Model. *Health Expectations*, 13, 73–85.

Verba, Sidney, Nie, Norman H., & Kim, Jae-On 1978. *Participation and Political Equality. A Seven-Nation Comparison*, New York: Cambridge University Press.

Verba, Sidney, Schlozman, Kay Lehman, & Brady, Henry E. 1995. *Voice and Equality. Civic Voluntarism in American Politics*, Cambridge, MA: Harvard University Press.

Wampler, Brian 2007. *Participatory Budgeting in Brazil. Contestation, Cooperation, and Accountability* University Park: The Pennsylvania State University Press.

Weitz-Shapiro, Rebecca. 2008. The Local Connection: Local Government Performance and Satisfaction With Democracy in Argentina. *Comparative Political Studies*, 41, 285–308.

Wendt, Claus, Frisina, Lorraine, & Rothgang, Heinz 2009. Healthcare System Types: A Conceptual Framework for Comparison. *Social Policy & Administration*, 43, 70–90.

Willis, Eliza, Garman, Christopher, & Haggard, Stephan 1999. The Politics of Decentralization in Latin America. *Latin American Research Review*, 34, 7–56.

Wolford, Wendy 2010. Participatory Democracy by Default: Land Reform, Social Movements and the State in Brazil. *Journal of Peasant Studies*, 37, 91–109.

World Health Organization 1978. *Declaration of Alma Ata*, Geneva: World Health Organization.

World Health Organization 2008. Portugal's Rapid Progress through Primary Health Care. *Bulletin of the World Health Organization*, 86, 826–827.

Zaremberg, Gisela 2012. "We're Either Burned or Frozen Out": Society and Party Systems in Latin American Municipal Development Councils (Nicaragua, Venezuela, Mexico, and Brazil). *In:* Cameron, Maxwell A., Hershberg, Eric, & Sharpe, Kenneth E. (eds.) *New Institutions for Participatory Democracy in Latin America. Voice and Consequence.* New York: Palgrave Macmillan, 21–51.

Zaremberg, Gisela, Isunza Vera, Ernesto, & Gurza Lavalle, Adrian 2017. The Gattopardo Era: Innovation and Representation in Mexico in Post-Neoliberal Times. *In:* Falleti, Tulia G. & Parrado, Emilio A. (eds.) *Latin America Since the Left Turn.* Philadelphia: The University of Pennsylvania Press, 264–282.

Acknowledgments

We are grateful to Luis Caiella, Luis Cecchi, Emmerich Davies, Galileu Kim, Yasmín Mertehikian, and Sara Niedzwiecki for their research assistance. We are also grateful to all the interviewees, who were exceedingly generous in sharing their knowledge about community participation, and to Carlos Anigstein and Federico Tobar, who also provided relevant documents and bibliography. Melani Cammett, Archon Fung, Merilee Grindle, Joseph Harris, Ben R. Schneider, the participants of the manuscript workshop at MIT, and two anonymous press reviewers provided very helpful comments on previous versions of this Element.

Cambridge Elements

Politics of Development

Melani Cammett
Harvard University

Melani Cammett is Clarence Dillon Professor of International Affairs in the Department of Government at Harvard University and Professor (secondary faculty appointment) in the Department of Global Health and Population in the Harvard T.H. Chan School of Public Health.

Ben Ross Schneider
Massachusetts Institute of Technology

Ben Ross Schneider is Ford International Professor of Political Science at MIT and Director of the MIT-Brazil program.

Advisory Board
Yuen Yuen Ang *University of Michigan*
Catherine Boone *London School of Economics*
Stephan Haggard *University of California, San Diego*
Prerna Singh *Brown University*
Dan Slater *University of Michigan*

About the series

The Element Series *Politics of Development* provides important contributions on both established and new topics on the politics and political economy of developing countries. A particular priority is to give increased visibility to a dynamic and growing body of social science research that examines the political and social determinants of economic development, as well as the effects of different development models on political and social outcomes.

Cambridge Elements ☰

Politics of Development

Elements in the series

Developmental States
Stephan Haggard

Coercive Distribution
Michael Albertus, Sofia Fenner and Dan Slater

A full series listing is available at: www.cambridge.org/EPOD

Printed in the United States
By Bookmasters